Armies of Celtic Europe
700 BC to AD 106

Armies of Celtic Europe
700 BC to AD 106

History, Organization
& Equipment

Gabriele Esposito

Pen & Sword
MILITARY

First published in Great Britain in 2019 by
Pen & Sword Military
An imprint of
Pen & Sword Books Ltd
Yorkshire – Philadelphia

ISBN 978 1 52673 033 6

A CIP catalogue record for this book is
available from the British Library

Typeset in Ehrhardt
by Mac Style

Printed and bound in India by Replika Press Pvt. Ltd.

Pen & Sword Books Limited incorporates the imprints of Atlas, Archaeology,
Aviation, Discovery, Family History, Fiction, History, Maritime, Military, Military
Classics, Politics, Select, Transport, True Crime, Air World, Frontline Publishing,
Leo Cooper, Remember When, Seaforth Publishing, The Praetorian Press,
Wharncliffe Local History, Wharncliffe Transport, Wharncliffe True Crime
and White Owl.

For a complete list of Pen & Sword titles please contact

PEN & SWORD BOOKS LIMITED
47 Church Street, Barnsley, South Yorkshire, S70 2AS, England
E-mail: enquiries@pen-and-sword.co.uk
Website: www.pen-and-sword.co.uk

Or

PEN AND SWORD BOOKS
1950 Lawrence Rd, Havertown, PA 19083, USA
E-mail: Uspen-and-sword@casematepublishers.com
Website: www.penandswordbooks.com

Contents

Gabriele Esposito is a military historian who works as a freelance author and researcher for some of the most important publishing houses in the military history sector. In particular, he is an expert specializing in uniformology: his interests and expertise range from the ancient civilizations to modern post-colonial conflicts. During recent years he has conducted and published several researches on the military history of the Latin American countries, with special attention on the War of the Triple Alliance and the War of the Pacific. He is among the leading experts on the military history of the Italian Wars of Unification and the Spanish Carlist Wars. His books and essays are published on a regular basis by Osprey Publishing, Winged Hussar Publishing and Libreria Editrice Goriziana; he is also the author of numerous military history articles appearing in specialized magazines like *Ancient Warfare Magazine*, *Medieval Warfare Magazine*, *The Armourer*, *History of War*, *Guerres et Histoire*, *Focus Storia* and *Focus Storia Wars*.

Acknowledgements

This book is dedicated to my fantastic parents, Maria Rosaria and Benedetto, for their great love and fundamental support in every phase of my life. Thanks to their precious words, the present book is a much better product: their great intelligence is always a secure harbour for me.

A very special mention goes to all the reenactment groups and living history associations who collaborated to this book, for providing me the magnificent and detailed photos that illustrate it: *Confraternita del Leone/Historia Viva*, *Contoutos Atrebates*, *G.A.S.A.C.*, *Les Ambiani*, *Les Mediomatrici*, *Les Trimatrici*, *Teuta Arverni* and *Teuta Osismi*. Without their incredible work of research and reenactment, the present work would have not been the same. I want to express my deep gratitude to all the leaders of these groups: they enjoyed and supported the idea of this book since the beginnings and helped me in every phase of the production with great generosity and patience.

Introduction

The Celts are without doubt one of the most important peoples of Antiquity, since they represent something extremely significant for the history of Europe. They were the first proper civilization appearing in the northern part of the continent, after centuries during which Continental Europe had been some steps behind Mediterranean Europe in terms of technological progress and cultural development. Their heritage had a deep impact on the development of the continent, as Celtic art and religion were among the most important expressions of early European civilization. If we look at the cultural and artistic traditions of modern Europe, the Celtic influence is still clearly visible: this is particularly true for those areas of the continent where Celtic civilization experienced a higher degree of continuity, like Ireland and Scotland or Wales and Brittany. In the ninth-eighth centuries BC, when the Celts started to emerge, various Mediterranean civilizations were flourishing at full speed: the most important of these was represented by the Greek world, which started to re-emerge from the so-called 'Hellenistic Middle Ages' that had followed the collapse of the Mycenean Civilization. The Greek cities were now increasing their populations and thus needed new markets for their growing economies: as a result, the necessities of commerce led the Greeks to the colonization of new territories that were located outside their homeland. In a few decades, Greek cities were founded in every corner of the Mediterranean, in a process that can be reasonably considered as the key factor behind the success of Greece during the later Classical Age. But the Greeks were not the only people living and expanding in the Mediterranean of the time: the Phoenicians, skilled merchants and famous seamen, were in the process of doing something very similar to Greek colonization. They started to settle across the Mediterranean in key locations, founding new colonies in territories like North Africa; it was in present-day Tunisia, for example, that they created the most important of their overseas cities: Carthage. The latter, during the following centuries, would become the most important commercial and military power of the western Mediterranean. Greeks and Carthaginians were not the only 'actors' of this age: in the East, Egypt and Assyria continued to be two of the largest military powers of the Ancient World; in the West, the Italic and Iberian civilizations started to become much more mature thanks to the influxes of the Greeks and Carthaginians. Those were the years during which Rome was founded, just a few decades after Carthage.

At this point, looking at the map of Europe, it would be easy to conclude that all the great civilizations were located in the southern and Mediterranean part of the continent. As a result, a very simple question would come to mind: what happened during those same years in Continental Europe? Who lived in the regions of present-day France and Great Britain? Until the eighth century BC, northern Europe continued to be characterized by a Bronze Age culture that could not be considered as a proper 'civilization'; all this changed with the development of the Celts, who soon became the first 'historical' people of Continental Europe. As a result, we could say that the proper history of many important European countries started with them. Across the centuries of their long history, the Celts came into contact with all the Mediterranean civilizations discussed above: they invaded and pillaged Greece, fought as mercenaries for Carthage, settled in the northern part of the Italian peninsula, mixed with the Iberians to create a new culture, went to Egypt to fight for the local rulers and even created a new state in Asia Minor. From this list of historical events, it is easy to understand how the Celts were great protagonists of Antiquity, who left their mark on many aspects of our actual life. Knowing Celtic history well means knowing the origins of European civilization: it would be wrong, in fact, to consider the latter only as the product of the Greek and Roman cultures. History is written by the victors, and the Celts did not produce any written account of their culture, but this does not mean that we should underestimate their great historical achievements.

Bearing in mind all the above, we could say that this book has a double aim: first of all, it wants to present the Celts as a 'unified' civilization of Europe. As we will see, the Celts were politically divided into a large number of autonomous tribes, living in different territories and frequently having contrasting interests. Across the centuries, they expanded themselves into most of Europe, conquering vast lands in Italy and Spain but also marching across the Balkans and Asia Minor: this, however, cannot cancel the fact that all Celtic tribes shared a common way of life. Celtic culture, art, religion, economy, society and warfare were all the same, from Ireland to Hungary. As a result, we will try to follow the general history of the Celts by presenting them as a 'unified' civilization that moved and lived across most of Europe. Following the single tribes in their migrations and campaigns would make little sense, since this could partly overshadow the importance of considering the Celts as a single people. The second aim of this book, as for all the other ones of this series, is to present a detailed analysis of Celtic warfare across the centuries, from the early warriors of the Late Bronze Age to the last defenders of Celtic freedom in the first century AD. As we will see, the Celtic warriors used very advanced military technologies: their weapons, at least initially, were superior to those of any Mediterranean civilization. The Celts, in fact, were real masters in working metals to produce deadly weapons or effective agricultural tools.

Their military technologies evolved greatly across the centuries, but always remained quite innovative (to the point that some of them, like chainmail, were copied by their Roman enemies). We will follow this evolutive process from the beginning to the end, taking into consideration the regional differences existing between various Celtic tribes. The Celts obviously had continuous contacts with other civilizations living at their borders, which meant that they sometimes adopted military equipment or tactics that were used by other peoples, since reciprocal influences were something natural.

Generally speaking, the Celts were a very warlike people: war was an extremely important component of their daily life and had strong links with the economic and religious activities of the various communities. Pillaging and raiding were normal practices in the Celtic world, with inter-tribal small wars being fought almost without interruption. Each skirmish or incursion into the territories of a bordering tribe represented a great opportunity for a Celtic warrior, who had as the main objective of his life that of showing his military valour to the community. Celtic religion and culture gave great importance to war, which was considered as a fundamental element of the world and not simply as an occasional activity. With the progression of time and the development of their civilization, the Celts gradually abandoned their early forms of warfare and started to conduct larger campaigns against new enemies. Expanding across Europe, they encountered different kinds of military opponents and thus had to partly change their own tactics in order to defeat the new enemies. Across the centuries, the Celts fought against Greek phalanxes, Roman legions, Etruscan hoplites, Germanic warriors and many other kinds of foes. On many occasions, they were able to win; on many others, however, the overall superiority of the enemy led them to defeat. The warlike nature of the Celts was not only related to their peculiar vision of the world, but also to very practical reasons. As we have already said, their mastery in producing weapons gave them a great technological advantage over the other contemporary civilizations; but the Celts also had something else that made them perfect warriors: their bodies, forged by a harsh way of life that was based on hard work in a difficult natural environment. The Continental Europe in which the Celts lived was very different from the Mediterranean one of the Greeks and Romans, being entirely covered with dense woods, where wild animals were still very numerous. There were no cities, except for the few coastal colonies founded by the Greeks and Phoenicians; mineral resources were abundant, but communications were quite difficult. To sum up, Celtic communities were scattered in small villages and had to work very hard in order to earn a living. This, combined with their genetic characteristics that gave them an impressive stature, made the Celts real 'war machines': they were much taller than the Greeks or Romans and could live on every kind of terrain, also with very little resources. As we will see in the pages of this book, all the enemies of the Celts had something in common: admiration for these courageous warriors coming from Continental Europe.

Chapter 1

The Origins of the Celts and the 'Hallstatt Culture'

A round 800/700 BC, Continental Europe was inhabited by different Indo-European communities: these did not have a common 'civilization' to speak of, but surely shared many characteristics. Gradually, since 1200 BC, the points of contact between these communities had become much more significant. A new common way of life started to spread across Central Europe, commonly known as 'Urnfield Culture', which is today considered as a sort of pre-Celtic phase of European history, during which the Indo-Europeans of Central Europe started to amalgamate themselves into a single and much more advanced civilization. This process lasted more or less four centuries and resulted in the emergence of Celtic culture. 'Urnfield Culture' derives its name from the fact that these proto-Celts cremated their dead and placed their bones into urns that were grouped into flat cemeteries. These Indo-Europeans are also known as 'Tumulus People', because they used to build impressive barrows over the tombs of their most prominent leaders. It is important to note, however, that the Indo-Europeans were not alone in Central Europe: they were the newcomers of that region, who lived among much more numerous communities of 'native' Europeans. The mass migrations of Indo-Europeans, in fact, had not overrun the peoples already inhabiting Europe before their arrival; these communities had a lower level of development if compared with the newcomers, but controlled most of the territory. Gradually, thanks to their superior technological skills (especially in working bronze), the Indo-Europeans were able to achieve a certain superiority over the 'natives' and started to subdue them. We know very little of this extremely ancient fusion, but there are no doubts that if the Indo-Europeans were able to prevail it was mostly thanks to their warlike nature. To sum up, the ancestors of the Celts were already skilled and well-equipped warriors (who used excellent bronze weapons). By 1200 BC, when the 'Urnfield Culture' started to develop and expand, the Indo-Europeans of Central Europe were much more numerous than before and now had more elements in common between them (in addition to language).

The tombs of the proto-Celts, dating back to 1000 BC, contain many swords of good quality, another important element that confirms the warlike nature of these communities. Recent studies of comparative linguistics have showed that the term 'Celts' could come from the Indo-European 'kel', a verb meaning 'to strike'. As a result, it is highly plausible that the term 'Celts' could derive from the fact that these ancient warriors were used to striking and fighting with swords. Their swords were superior weapons for the time, never seen before by the 'native' peoples living around the proto-Celts; apparently these swords were so effective that they gave the name to the warriors using them. In general, at least at the beginning, we could say that the word 'Celt' meant 'warrior/man who strikes with a sword'. The proto-Celts also had some other advantages over the 'native' communities living around them: for example, they used horses for transportation to a larger extent than the other ancient

Celtic heavy cavalryman with the head of a killed enemy; he is not using the usual "horned" saddle of the Celtic cavalry, which provided good stability to the rider. (the *Mediomatrici*)

Celtic heavy infantryman with chainmail. (*Antichi Popoli/Confraternita del Leone*)

Europeans. This higher level of mobility had very positive consequences over trade and commerce. We don't know if the proto-Celts already used horse-drawn chariots in battle, but it is plausible that these were another key factor determining their military superiority. The warriors of the 'Urnfield Culture' had to fight for centuries in order to acquire predominance over Central Europe: obviously the experiences of this long period were extremely important in determining the basic characteristics of the future Celtic civilization. The culture, religion and art of the Celts were always influenced by the kind of daily life conducted by these courageous warriors. Once supremacy was achieved, the proto-Celts could create more permanent settlements and thus start to develop a much more complex civilization. By 800 BC, the time had come for the beginning of a new phase in European history (the first one of the Celtic civilization), known as 'Hallstatt Culture'. This started to develop in present-day Austria, but very soon the Celts expanded their new civilization across the Alps, reaching Switzerland/ France in the west and Hungary in the east.

Hallstatt is a small village located in the mountains of Austria (near Salzburg) that has become famous due to the rich Celtic burials that were found on its territory (in the proximity of a lake) during the nineteenth century, and were of great importance to understanding and reconstructing the way of life of the early Celts. The name of the village, like for many other important archaeological sites of Europe, contains the term 'halle' that was usually related to the presence of salt on the territory. Salt was the equivalent of gold during the Bronze Age and even before, thus playing a key role in commerce and trading. As a result, possessing a salt mine could determine the fortunes of a community. Salt was a source of wealth and a fundamental element in the daily life of the time, being precious enough to be traded for other goods (like metal weapons) and universally used to preserve food. The early Celtic communities of Austria grew rich thanks to the salt trade and soon started to expand their political influence towards bordering territories. In only a few decades their area of control reached the Rhine on the frontier of modern France and the Danube on the western border of Hungary. During these early centuries, however, Austria and Switzerland remained the core of the Celtic territories: the Alps were rich in mineral resources, which the Celts needed in order to maintain their commercial supremacy over other peoples. At the time of the 'Hallstatt Culture', bronze was still the dominant metal, not being fully replaced by iron for some centuries, during which time the Celts continued to produce large amounts of weapons and tools in bronze. The Celtic artisans were masters in producing arms and armours in bronze, which was obtained quite simply by combining tin and copper. The weapons produced by the 'Hallstatt Culture' were not only extremely effective, but also had very nice decorations. The Celtic warriors of this period were not used to large-scale military operations, usually fighting only to protect their commercial interests: short-term raids and incursions were most common. All the Celtic tribes were essentially communities of farmers, which were used to increasing the number of their animals by robbing those of their neighbours, meaning the main function of warriors was that of defending cattle from enemy raiders.

Obviously, from these early times, Celtic society started to present a series of stratifications: each free man was a warrior, but not all men were on the same social level. Those who controlled the mines (of salt or of metals) and the largest cattle herds formed a sort of aristocracy, and these nobles were rich enough to have a full panoply of highly decorated bronze weapons and could also have large numbers of slaves at their service. Slaves were usually captured enemies, mostly employed as workers in the mines, who could be bought and sold like any other goods of the time. Thanks to the strategic position of their settlements in the Alps, the Celts could trade both with the other peoples of Continental Europe (living in the north) and with the more advanced Mediterranean civilizations of the south (in Italy and Greece). The Celts sold salt, metals and slaves in exchange for luxury goods like wine. In addition, they could sell the products coming from the south to the peoples living north of their settlements (thus exerting a sort of control over the distribution of these costly products). Celtic warriors of the 'Hallstatt Culture' were equipped quite differently from those of the following centuries, whose weapons would become famous thanks to their deadly encounters with the Greeks and Romans. As already stated, arms and armours were mostly made of bronze and had important ritual functions in addition to their practical ones. It is important to note that, with the progression of time, bronze started to be mixed with iron in order to produce stronger weapons, but the addition of the new material did not greatly change the general patterns of Celtic arms and armours. A noble warrior of the 'Hallstatt Culture' would have been fully equipped with helmet, cuirass, shield, sword and spear: each of these elements was produced in a different way and could be of different models. These models changed very little during the whole period of the 'Hallstatt Culture', which lasted more or less for three centuries (from 800-500 BC). At the beginning of the sixth century BC, a new phase of Celtic civilization began and the Celts started to move across Europe with the objective of conquering new territories.

In total, the Celtic burials found around the site of Hallstatt are more or less 2,000: an impressive number for the standards of the Late Bronze Age, which makes Hallstatt one of the most important archaeological sites of the world. These burials were different from those of the previous period, since they did not contain urns with cremated bodies but wooden chambers with wagons (with the bodies inside). Thanks to the numerous weapons that were found in the burials, we are able to have a quite precise reconstruction of the weapons used by the early Celtic warriors. Generally speaking, the eighth century was a period of transition from a technological point

Celtic heavy infantryman with full heavy equipment. (*Antichi Popoli / Confraternita del Leone*)

Celtic swordsman with chainmail. (*Antichi Popoli / Confraternita del Leone*)

of view, seeing the progressive passage from the Late Bronze Age to the Early Iron Age. The arms and armour discovered at Hallstatt are a sort of 'photograph' that reproduces this important passage from one metal to another, as a result of which many scholars consider the weapons and tools found at Hallstatt to be a symbol of the new era that was approaching (the Early Iron Age). What we know for sure is that the case of Hallstatt was not a single one: in many other key locations of Central Europe, like Heuneburg in Germany, the Celts built partly fortified villages in order to control the local commercial routes and exploit natural resources that were located on the territory. During this period of their history, the Celts did not produce figurative art, so the arms and armour found in burials are the only elements we have to reconstruct their weaponry. In addition, before their expansion that began into the fifth century BC, the contacts of the Celts with other populations remained sporadic enough to prevent the latter from writing detailed accounts of the northern warriors. As already said, the weapons of each Celtic warrior reflected his social status and his personal wealth: a noble could have full equipment and could go to battle mounted on a chariot, while a simple farmer would generally be equipped with just a helmet and his offensive weapons.

Military organization of these early Celtic communities was very simple and reflected their social structure: the warriors from each small village, who were all part of families that were linked between them, had to defend the properties and interests of their clan. Each community was ruled by a prominent leader, coming from the richest or most powerful family of the village. These nobles were responsible for the destinies of the farms that were under their control, but were also traders who wanted to earn as much as possible from their commercial activities. The free men of each community had to fight at the orders of their respective leaders, but generally speaking the average Celtic man had a very independent character: he would have fought to defend his territory or to launch raids against bordering tribes, but would have been very reluctant to fight only for protecting the commercial interests of his warlord. As a result of this situation, bearing in mind that the woods of Central Europe were the ideal places to organize ambushes against convoys transporting goods, it is reasonable to suppose that some sort of professional full-time warriors had to exist. The noble warlords/merchants surely felt the need to have a core of permanent fighters who could escort their commercial convoys coming from or directed to the south of the Alps. In addition, the key mountain passes and fortified positions controlled by each noble had to be garrisoned in a stable way. To sum up, it is very plausible that some sort of professional Celtic warriors existed since the period of the 'Hallstatt Culture'; these were at the service of the nobles and acted as their personal bodyguards, performing a huge variety of different functions. Obviously, being paid for their services, these were rich enough to have good personal equipment. The defence of their warlord's properties and the escort of commercial convoys were the main tasks performed by these skilled warriors, but we should not forget that each Celtic noble was also a warrior chief who had to guide his men during the incursions and raids against bordering villages. When the small 'army' of each community was assembled for such offensive operations, the professional warriors were supplemented by the farmers (who had less military experience but the same desire to pillage as much as possible). We don't know if the small Celtic 'armies' of these times already comprised different troop types, yet due to the differences existing in their respective equipments, we could say that the nobles and their professional warriors formed a sort of heavy infantry while the other part-time fighters could be considered as light infantrymen.

Regarding mounted troops, we have very few details. During later periods, the Celts used both war chariots and simple horses in battle, but for this early period we have no precise accounts detailing Celtic battle tactics and thus we cannot confirm the employment of chariots and horses. War chariots have been found in some burials, but we don't know if these were simply used as ceremonial means of transport or as a sort of heavy cavalry (as it was in later times). Celtic horses were quite small and thus could not be used by a 'shock' cavalry to charge in close order: as a result, at least for these early times, it is reasonable to presume that the Celts employed horses at war only for secondary purposes (like reconnaissance and scouting). The fact that most of Central Europe was covered by woods was another element determining only little use of horses for warfare. The convoys transporting goods from southern to northern Europe surely had some form of mounted escorts, but these were probably composed of just a few horsemen: foreign merchants who travelled across the lands of a Celtic warlord had to pay them for the services of such escorts. In any case, convoys moved very slowly and thus could be easily protected by foot warriors.

During the centuries of the 'Hallstatt Culture', Celtic armour consisted of three different elements: cuirass, waistbelt and greaves (all made of bronze). The cuirass was worn by the richest warriors of each community, while the waistbelt was an alternative form of body protection used by those who were wealthy but not enough to have a cuirass. The greaves were not very common and were generally employed only by those warriors who also wore a cuirass. The latter had a quite simple shape and covered the torso (front and back). It could be decorated with a huge variety of geometrical motifs, which were reproduced thanks to the presence of little studs and incisions (the position of which determined the shape of the motifs). The cuirass was quite heavy, but gave excellent protection to any warrior wearing it. There was no protection for the arms, which enabled the Celtic warriors to use their offensive weapons with no limitations of any sort. This original pattern of cuirass was used

Celtic warlord with 'Negau' helmet. (*Antichi Popoli / Confraternita del Leone*)

Celtic nobleman with heavy armour. (the *Ambiani*)

from the beginning of the 'Hallstatt Culture' and remained popular during all the period taken into account. However, from the sixth century BC, the Celts started to have much more frequent contacts with the Mediterranean civilizations, which had a certain influence over their military equipment. A new kind of cuirass was introduced, together with some use of the greaves (which remained quite limited, because Celtic warriors always avoided using elements that could limit their mobility in battle). The new model of cuirass derived from the contemporary Greek 'bell cuirass' (used by the first hoplite formations), which derived its name from the fact that it was bell-shaped (being larger in the bottom part) and had as its main characteristic that of reproducing (albeit in a very naive way) the anatomy of the torso. These simple decorative incisions, sometimes integrated with studs, were still very elementary: later, in the Greek world, they would evolve into the 'muscle cuirass' employed by the hoplites. In general, the 'bell cuirass' was not so different from the traditional Celtic one, except for being larger in the bottom part, and this similarity led to the progressive fusion of the two models, with traditional cuirasses presenting anatomic incisions and 'bell cuirasses' geometrical motifs made with bosses.

The greaves were quite simple and had no particular decorations. They were rectangular in shape and larger in the area covering the knees. Celtic warriors of this period wore shoes or boots made with leather: the former were very simple and were worn when using greaves, while the latter reached to the knee and were very hard-wearing, having lacing on the frontal part. Greaves could not be worn together with boots. Waistbelts were quite large and had the same geometrical decorations as the cuirasses, with incisions and bosses. Like most of the ancient peoples deriving from the Indo-Europeans, the Celts wore such bronze waistbelts as a form of social distinction: only free men could use them in time of war and thus they had an important symbolic function. They gave to their wearer some sort of protection for the waist, but could not be compared to a cuirass. Unfortunately, only sets of bronze armour have survived from the Hallstatt period, so we don't know if the Celts from this age also employed personal protection made from organic materials like leather (which unlike metals do not survive for centuries). Most scholars, however, agree that the 'ordinary' Celtic warriors probably wore some leather cuirasses: these would have been cheaper and easier to produce than the bronze ones, so their use could have been very common. These 'organic' cuirasses were presumably longer than the bronze ones (which did not continue under the waistbelt), and possibly had reinforcements made of bronze (like small bosses). Maybe they could be made of padded material to offer a better defence.

Celtic helmets from this period could be of two main different kinds, each having some distinctive features that made them easily recognizable. The most ancient and probably most popular of these was the 'crested helmet': this was domed in the

Celtic swordsman with full heavy equipment. (the *Ambiani*)

Celtic noble warrior with lorica hamata. (the *Ambiani*)

bottom part but had a tall crest on the top, which was made of bronze like the rest of the helmet. Both the bottom part and the crest were pointed, being decorated by many small bosses. The crest was placed transversely on the helmet, dividing it in two symmetrical parts and running across it in correspondence with the nose of the wearer. The bottom part of the helmet was reinforced by an external ridge and was generally decorated with three horizontal rows of bosses. The crest did not reach the external ridge in the bottom part: the surface separating these two components of the helmet was covered by six protruding strips of bronze (three on the front and three on the back of the helmet). The crest mostly had a decorative function, since it made the warriors look taller than they actually were, but also offered some additional protection from slashing blows coming from above. The 'crested helmet' of the Celts was also copied and adopted by other peoples, like the Etruscans of central Italy who employed it on a large scale during the early phases of their civilization. Apparently these helmets had an important symbolic function, since they have been found in large numbers both in Celtic and Etruscan tombs, which suggests that 'crested helmets' were considered as a 'parade' object and not as proper 'war' helmets. The truth is probably between the two: initially they were surely used in combat, but as time progressed it is reasonable to think that for practical purposes they were replaced by simpler models of helmet. Regardless, they gradually became an iconic element of the Celtic panoply, which became especially popular in the Italian peninsula. It is highly probable that the early warriors of Rome, in the eighth century BC, wore exactly this kind of helmet.

The second kind of helmet, which would later evolve into the so-called 'Negau helmet', consisted of a pot-shaped bottom part having a wide brim around its base and two transversal ridges on the top that were surmounted by a large crest made of horsehair. This kind of helmet, known as 'double ridge' or 'Buckelhelm', could be decorated with sculpted figures on its external surface (generally reproducing sacred animals) or with bosses on the brim. The dimensions of the latter and of the crest could vary a lot; in general, however, this kind of helmet was much more practical to wear than the 'crested' one and its brim gave additional protection to the face of the wearer (for example from arrows coming from above). Like the latter, it was also quite popular in other parts of Europe (such as Italy or the Balkans). As time progressed, both the 'crested helmet' and 'double ridge helmet' became much simpler: the dimensions of the former's crest were strongly reduced, while the brim of the latter's became increasingly smaller. At the end of this evolutive process, both the crest and brim disappeared from their respective models of helmet.

The defensive equipment of the early Celtic warriors was completed by the shield, which could be hexagonal or oval in shape. We don't have any surviving representation of shields from this period, so we can just suppose that the latter were similar to those

Celtic warlords with heavy armour. (the *Ambiani*)

that were used during later periods (which will be discussed later). Since no metal components of shields have survived from the Hallstatt age, we can suppose that the early shields employed during this period were entirely made of wood and other organic materials.

The main offensive weapons were spear and sword, but these could be supplemented by javelins and daggers. The spear was used for thrusting, while javelins were employed from distance and were designed for being thrown. The sword, which was quite long, was mostly used for slashing (being particularly deadly when employed by mounted warriors), and the dagger had a very tapered point and was ideal for use in close combat. The design of the spear's point was very simple but quite effective, remaining practically the same for centuries. The blade had the shape of a willow-tree leaf and

Celtic warlord with full heavy equipment. (the *Trimatrici*)

was reinforced by a central ridge. It could be made of bronze or iron, but the latter material became increasingly popular as time progressed. The use of spears with iron points gave the Celts a great advantage over their enemies: iron could easily pierce a cuirass made of bronze or a shield made of wood. The javelins' heads had the same basic shape as the spears' points, but with no central ridge and were obviously smaller. Javelins were used from distance during the early phases of a combat, being decisive on rare occasions.

The Celtic swords produced by the 'Hallstatt Culture' were in many aspects similar to later ones, but were produced with different methods. In general, at the beginning of the period taken into account the majority of swords were still made of bronze; as time progressed, however, iron became the most popular metal for constructing such weapons. Most Celtic fighting was conducted with swords, since spears usually broke after the first or second thrust; as a result, the sword was the most important and highly symbolic element of each warrior's personal equipment. As we have seen, bronze was replaced by iron in the production of every military component. The first piece of equipment that started to be made of iron were swords, followed by the points of spears. The Celts soon understood that by using long slashing swords with iron blades, they could easily defeat any kind of enemy: as a result, bronze was abandoned more rapidly for the production of swords than for any other kind of metal production. Early Iron Age swords were work-hardened rather than quench-hardened, and thus were still quite similar in terms of quality to the bronze ones of the Late Bronze Age. Unlike later swords, they could easily break during combat or change shape when hitting some harder material.

The general design of Hallstatt swords was clearly based upon that of the previous flange-hilted swords of the Late Bronze Age; the long blade was leaf-shaped and had a broad neck, with the greatest width being generally low down towards the point. The ricasso (the unsharpened length of blade just above the handle of the sword) was very short and had a notch that varied greatly in depth. The point of the blade terminated in a distinctive blunt triangular form, the sides of which were drawn at an angle of 45 degrees to the axis of the blade. The shape of the point clearly demonstrates that these weapons were used for slashing and not for thrusting. The tang of these swords (the internal part of the handle, made of metal but covered with organic material) swells sharply, to a point of greatest width that is placed just below its centre. Differently from the previous swords of the Late Bronze Age, these blades had tangs without flanges; despite this, some sort of flanged effect was sometimes produced by a slight dishing located along the edges of the tang. The handle had a crossguard with 'sloping shoulders' shape and was completed by a pommel, which was connected to the tang thanks to a rivet-hole. The blades were sharpened on both sides and could be

Celtic nobleman with chainmail. (The *Ambiani*)

Celtic swordsman with heavy equipment. (The *Ambiani*)

decorated with incisions of various kinds, which generally reproduced geometrical motifs. Hallstatt swords have been traditionally divided into two groups: a longer variety known as 'Mindelheim Type' and a shorter one called 'Gundlingen Type'. Swords of both types were transported in bronze or iron scabbards, richly decorated with incisions and/or bosses (like the handles); these were attached to a leather belt or a chain made of bronze/iron. The terminal part of scabbards was generally enriched by the presence of decorative sculptures. Daggers were very short but had quite large blades (which presented a central ridge, acting as reinforcement) and could have different models of handle (the latter was generally decorated with 'antennae', which were rounded horns). All daggers had a triangular point, which made them a deadly weapon when used in close combat (especially if employed to thrust in those parts of the enemy's body that were not protected by armour). In addition to daggers, hatchets with a simple bronze or iron blade could also be used as secondary offensive weapons.

Chapter 2

The 'La Tène Culture' and Early Celtic Expansion

Around 500 BC, while Greece was at war with the Persian Empire and Rome was struggling to become a Republic after having been ruled by kings, the Celts of Central Europe started to develop a new culture that would correspond to the second and most important phase of their history. This is commonly known as 'La Tène Culture': like the previous Hallstatt one, its name derives from the main archaeological site where important remnants of this culture were found. The 'Hallstatt Culture' had been initially centred on Austria, but over time had expanded across the Alps. By 500 BC, the whole territory of Switzerland had been absorbed into the Celtic sphere of influence: the Celts had reached the Rhine in the west and the Danube in the east, but their core territories were still in the Alps. At the beginning of the sixth century BC, something started to change, as the Celts developed a new, superior culture that enabled them to expand much more rapidly and permanently than before. 'La Tène' meant 'shallow waters' in the Celtic language, and the site bearing this name is located on the north side of Lake Neuchatel in Switzerland. This place surely had an important religious meaning for the Celts, because here they made their rich offerings to the gods in the form of weapons and other objects that were deposited in the lake. The site was first discovered in 1857 when the water level of the lake dropped, but most of the objects were collected only during the period 1906-17. Thanks to these numerous and precious finds, it has been possible to understand the differences existing between this new culture and the previous Hallstatt one. First of all, the Celts of La Tène had different burial rites from their ancestors: nobles were now buried in light two-wheeled chariots rather than heavy four-wheeled wagons. In addition, the various objects from this new phase of Celtic history show a completely different artistic style. The art of the 'Hallstatt Culture' had been characterized by static and mostly geometric decorations, while the new one of the 'La Tène Culture' featured many movement-based forms. Most of the weapons and other objects were now decorated with inscribed and inlaid interlace or spirals, which were quite intricate. These elements would soon become an iconic component of Celtic art. The famous neck rings known as 'torques' and the elegant brooches known as 'fibulae' started to be produced on a massive scale during this period, becoming objects of universal use in the Celtic world. Stylized and curvilinear forms, representing sacred animals or

Celtic noble/rich warlord. (The *Ambiani*)

Celtic heavy infantryman with full equipment. (The *Mediomatrici*)

vegetal elements, started to be reproduced on many artefacts. By now, Celtic art was no longer based on abstract motifs, but tried to reproduce the natural world with a clear religious point of view. As pointed out by most scholars who have studied it, the 'La Tène Culture' was a result of the continuous cultural and commercial contacts that the Celts had with the Mediterranean world: Greek, Etruscan and Roman influences all contributed to the development of this new phase of Celtic civilization. The trade routes crossing Europe, already in existence before 500 BC, became much more important after that date, and as a result the Celts started to export salt, tin, copper, amber, wool, leather, furs and gold to most of the Ancient world.

Thanks to their flourishing economy and great military capabilities, the Celts could start moving from their original home territories located in the Alps of Central Europe. One of their first targets was the territories of modern France, which lay west of the original Celtic world. Before the arrival of the Celts, France was inhabited by Indo-European populations sharing many common tracts with the 'Hallstatt Culture', of whom we know very little because, like the Celts, they left no written accounts of their history. For the Celts we can count on the historical works written by their Greek and Roman enemies, while for the pre-Celtic peoples of France we have nothing because neither the conquered nor the conquerors had a proper written alphabet. In any case, judging from archaeological finds, the pre-Celtic populations living in France had an inferior and older level of civilization if compared with the new La Tène one of the invaders. This was particularly apparent in the production processes employed to fabricate weapons and other metal tools. The Celts arrived in the territories of France from Switzerland by crossing the Rhine, and in a few decades, following the main waterways, they occupied the entire region and reached the Atlantic. The 'Celticization' of France lasted more or less a century (the fifth BC) and had enormous importance for the history of Europe: by the end of this process, the core centres of Celtic civilization had moved from the Alps to the plains of France, with the latter becoming known as Gaul from the term used by the Romans to identify Celts. Apparently, the fact that the Celts had a superior level of civilization made their fusion with the local pre-Celtic peoples quite easy; in addition, both the original populations and the newcomers shared a common background represented by the 'Hallstatt Culture'. Not all the territories of France, however, were inhabited by pre-Celtic peoples having the same levels of civilization: the northern part of the country had experienced very limited contacts with the Mediterranean world and thus was less developed than the southern one. The latter had been widely influenced by the Greeks, Phoenicians and Etruscans, who had all conducted commercial activities with the local communities. The Greeks, in particular, had founded their rich colony of Massalia (modern Marseille) on the Mediterranean coast of southern France. This Greek city, established around 600 BC, soon acquired a prominent role in the commercial system of the time. Thanks to its strategic position, Massalia could be the perfect link between France's populations and the Mediterranean civilizations. This situation did not change with the arrival of the Celts, who needed a port that could be used to export their products but could also import the large amounts of luxury goods coming from the south that they needed. The Celts were always in search of Mediterranean products like wine or oil. Being a 'mediator' between two different areas of Europe, Massalia became increasingly rich and important from a political point of view. Initially, the Greeks maintained good relations with the Celtic tribes living around them and expanded their cultural influence over much of southern France (by creating a commercial network that would last for centuries). As time progressed, the Celtic tribes living in Gaul started to assume a much more stable internal asset, with the whole territory inhabited by dozens of different communities, each of which controlled a precise region. As usual for the Celts, these tribes were almost constantly at war against each other: alliances between them changed very frequently and some more powerful ones gradually started to emerge (assuming control over smaller tribes and forming confederations). Gaul comprised all the territories of present-day France, plus most of modern Belgium and some lands on the eastern bank of the Rhine (in what is today Germany). The Pyrenees to the south and the Rhine to the east/north marked the borders of Gaul. At this time the Celts were not yet considered as 'barbarians' by the Greeks and Romans, whose contacts with the Gauls had always remained very positive. As we will see in the next chapter, this situation was going to change in a dramatic and definitive way.

During the fifth century bc, the Celts also started to move in other directions. After crossing the Alps, they marched south and gradually began to settle in northern Italy, which, similarly to pre-Celtic Gaul, was inhabited by Indo-European populations having many elements in common with the 'Hallstatt Culture'. This was particularly true for the Alpine areas, while the large plains of northern Italy were characterized by the much more advanced 'Villanovian Culture' and were part of the Etruscans' sphere of influence (the latter had their most important cities in Tuscany). The penetration of the Celts in Italy had two main phases: during the first, the newcomers had no great difficulties in occupying the mountain areas and in mixing with the local population; during the second, however, the Celts had to fight against the Etruscans in order to obtain control over the fertile and rich plains of northern Italy. The Celts of Italy also had to face another two enemies, the Ligurians and the Veneti, two peoples living on the coasts of ancient northern Italy. The Ligurians inhabited the eastern tract of the coast, from the western Alps to the Etruscan territories in Tuscany, while the Veneti were settled on the western tract of the coast, from the Po (the river which marked the northern border of the Etruscan world) to the eastern Alps. Both these peoples

Celtic swordsman with *lorica hamata*. (The *Mediomatrici*)

Example of Celtic chainmail armour. (The *Mediomatrici*)

had a higher level of civilization than the other Indo-European communities living in northern Italy: the Celts were gradually able to absorb them, but they always retained most of their distinctive cultural features (until their final conquest by the Romans). In other areas of northern Italy, however, Celtic predominance became absolute. The first Celtic incursions into northern Italy apparently took place as early as 600 BC, yet it was only during the fifth century BC that the Celtic presence in Italy became stable. While we could say that the 'Celticization' of France and northern Italy happened more or less during the same decades, the further Celtic expansion into western Europe, directed through the British Isles and Spain, took place in a subsequent phase. It is important to remember, however, that the Celts of the 'La Tène Culture' did not expand only across the western part of Europe: moving from Austria, they gradually also occupied large territories in the eastern part of the continent. Most of the modern Czech Republic and Slovakia were 'Celticized', as well as large portions of south-western Poland and western Hungary. The Celts would later also move into the northern Balkans (settling in modern Slovenia and Croatia) as well as other eastern areas located north of the Danube (such as Transylvania and western Ukraine). As is clear from the above, the Celts never expanded into the territories of present-day Germany, which were already inhabited by the strong proto-Germanic tribes of the so-called 'Jastorf Culture'. The Germans, who were completely different from the Celts in many ways, clashed with the latter on several occasions, and thus the reciprocal influences existing between the two peoples were quite rare. The Rhine to the west and the Danube to the south marked the border existing between the world of the Germans and that of the Celts. As we will see in subsequent chapters, the Germans gradually became a strong menace for the Celts and started to expand by attempting to conquer some of their territories. In general terms, we could say that the famous Roman '*limes*' created during the early Principate had already existed since Celtic times. The Germans always retained their separate identity, while the Celtic world was conquered and gradually absorbed into the Roman Empire. The Rhine and Danube continued to mark frontiers until the fifth century AD, when the Germans invaded most of Europe.

At this point it is important to describe how these Celtic communities from the 'La Tène' period lived and how they were organized from a social point of view. Basically, each free Celtic man was a farmer, in line with the social model of all the Indo-European peoples. The farmers made up the largest of the four categories that comprised Celtic society, the other three being the aristocracy of the rich warriors, the religious caste of the priests (the famous druids) and the slaves. The various farms of a settlement and the communities living in them were all grouped around a hill fort owned by a warlord. Celtic hill forts were not only fortified places, but also the centres from which various political leaders controlled the lives of farmers living under their control/protection.

Celtic swordsman with decorated leather armour. (The *Osismi*)

Celtic spearman with organic armour. (The *Atrebates*)

The size and extent of the fortifications were determined by the personal power of the aristocrats who owned them: some extended for just a few acres and protected a few hundred huts, while others could cover hundreds of acres and contain thousands of huts. Defences could range from a simple rampart-and-ditch structure to much more complex defensive systems made of stone. Hill forts could be used on a permanent basis or be employed only in time of war (when the population needed defence). They were built to protect not only the farmers but also their precious animals. The fact that the Celts were great warriors and raiders should not overshadow that they were also very capable peasants: agriculture and breeding were their main activities in time of peace, the first being mostly based on the production of cereals and the latter on specific animals (horses, cows, poultry and sheep). Not all Celtic free men, however, were farmers/peasants, a minority being artisans who practised productive activities that were fundamental for their society, the most important being weaving, potting, charcoal-burning and metal-smelting. Slaves could be owned by each free man, but obviously the noble warlords had large numbers of them. Slaves were usually captured enemies and were particularly precious, because they could be employed intensively to perform every kind of labour (in farms or to help artisans in their work).

The druids were separated from the rest of the population and were probably the most important group of Celtic society. The religion of the Celts was based on their belief that objects and the natural environment surrounding them were all pervaded by magical entities, influencing the daily lives of men and determining the destiny of each individual. Rituals and sacrifices were the most common practices of Celtic religion, and had as their main function that of placating the various magical entities in order to receive a better treatment in daily life. Sacred myths and tales were extremely common and popular, being a tool in the hands of the druids, who could use popular superstition to increase their personal power and influence the political life of their communities. Many of these myths and tales, based on the figures of heroic warriors and magic/natural elements, survived to the collapse of the Celtic world and thus have influenced European culture/imagery for several centuries. Religion was practised by all members of Celtic society and was strongly linked to the daily life of farmers and warriors. There were many collective rituals, all related to the natural seasons (from an agricultural point of view) or to war. Deities were an important component of Celtic religion, but they were not organized according to a very precise structure like for the Greeks or Romans. Like all the Indo-European peoples, the Celts had some major gods who were respected across the whole Celtic world, but also minor deities who were strongly linked to local communities (they could be related to a river or a mountain, for example). Most of them were usually represented as animals, since these played an important part in Celtic religion (being sacred and respected). The

Celtic warlord with transverse crest on the helmet (in Roman style). (The *Teuta Arverni*)

Celtic warrior with personal equipment carried in Roman style. (The *Teuta Arverni*)

priestly class of the druids was in charge of conducting all the rituals and sacrifices, but also had other important functions. They were not only magicians responsible for the religious life of their community, but also 'judges' who were called to act as arbitrators in case of disputes. Blood-feuds, frequently related to the ancestry of families, were extremely common and could cause major bloodshed without the direct intervention of a priest. Apparently, thanks to their special personal preparation and great knowledge, the druids could perform both these functions in a very effective way. They were the real guardians of Celtic culture and religion, which was mostly oral and thus had to be transmitted to the younger generations in order to be preserved. In essence, the druids were the proper 'ruling class' of the Celtic world (much more so than the rich warlords).

Celtic religion included some practices that looked particularly 'barbarian' to the Greeks and Romans, such as head-hunting or human sacrifices. The latter was common among the various Indo-European peoples, having also been practised by the Greeks and Romans during the early phases of their history. Head-hunting, however, was something peculiar to the Celtic vision of the world: the Celts were convinced that the head of a man (possibly a warrior) contained his personal 'life force' (a mixture of his mind, spirit, will and strength). As a result, collecting heads of dead enemies was a way for Celtic warriors to increase their personal capabilities: each head would have passed its 'vital energy' to its new owner. In addition to human and animal sacrifices, the Celts also practised them with weapons, consisting of votive deposits of arms and armours, especially if captured from a defeated enemy. Thanks to this peculiar religious practice, archaeologists have been able to find hundreds of Celtic swords in a very good state of conservation. The 'sacrificed' spoils could also include other metal tools, but weapons (together with war chariots) had a very important symbolic value. These votive deposits could be found on specifically consecrated ground as well as in lakes or marshes.

Head-hunting and human sacrifices were not the only elements of the Celtic world that impressed the Greeks and Romans. Another fundamental aspect was the physical appearance of these northern warriors, who were much taller than the average Mediterranean man of the time and had an impressive musculature. Their completely white skin, blue eyes and blonde/red hair formed a combination rarely seen in southern Europe. The daily life of an average Celtic farmer/warrior was characterized by many activities that favoured the development of a certain athleticism, while some practices – like that of styling wavy/curly hair with lime in order to whiten it – increased the Mediterranean perception of the Gauls as wild creatures coming from a mostly unknown world. The Celtic warriors knew this very well and thus left their abundant hair uncut, in order to draw it back from the forehead and make it look like a

Celtic infantryman with quilted armour. (The *Teuta Arverni*)

Celtic warriors with organic armour. (The *Ambiani*)

white mane of a horse. Long beards and drooping moustaches were also very popular, together with the use of clothes having bright colours, generally decorated with geometric motifs, which would gradually transform themselves into a sort of 'proto-Tartan'. Unlike the Greeks and Romans, all Celtic men wore trousers, a revolutionary piece of clothing for the time because they gave great protection from cold during winter (something particularly appreciated in Continental Europe) but were also very comfortable to wear when riding a horse. Over time, the Romans adopted trousers on a massive scale and exported their use throughout the Empire. The Mediterranean peoples were particularly impressed by the multi-coloured fabric that the Gauls used to produce their trousers, which was decorated with chequered and striped patterns that they had never seen before. During spring and summer, most of the Celtic men wore only trousers; during autumn and winter these were supplemented by tunics and cloaks. Tunics could have long or short sleeves, while cloaks could include large parts made of fur in order to offer better protection from cold temperatures. Both tunics and the cloaks were usually ornamented with braiding and fringes in contrasting colours, which were produced separately and later attached to the clothing. Obviously, as with arms and armours, the social status and personal wealth of each individual was reflected in the quality of the clothing worn: noble and rich warriors wore tunics and cloaks with heavy decorations, while poorer peasants/farmers could afford only simple clothes with solid colours and no ornamentations. Footwear consisted of simple leather shoes, as opposed to Mediterranean peoples who preferred wearing sandals. Jewellery was extremely popular and had a highly symbolic value: wearing a torque around the neck marked being a Celtic man, since this kind of jewel was a real mark of distinction in the ancient world. Neck rings could be made of gold, silver or bronze according to the wealth of their owners, with most of the golden and silver ones decorated with highly detailed incisions. Brooches, used to fix long cloaks on the shoulder, were another extremely common component of Celtic jewellery.

Celtic military organization did not change greatly during the 'La Tène' period if compared with that of the 'Hallstatt'. Celtic armies were never structured on regular military units like the Greek phalanxes or Roman legions. Military contingents continued to be raised according to their tribal/familiar origins, being strongly linked to the clan to which they belonged. When the leader of a Celtic tribe decided to go to war, all the free men living under his protection had to serve: as a result, the farmers/warriors left their homes and assembled at the hill fort of their warlord. Some military leaders were powerful and rich enough to be named kings and thus controlled very large territories. In the event of war mobilization, all the minor aristocrats living on the leader's land had to assemble their tribal contingents and thus join their overlord in order to form a sort of 'royal army'. Celtic military organization was highly influenced

Celtic warlord with leather cuirass. (The *Ambiani*)

Celtic warlord with leather armour. (The *Ambiani*)

by social structures and was based on solid personal relationships existing between the upper class of nobles and the large community of peasants/farmers. In case of raids or incursions against bordering tribes, free men could decide to join their warlord with the hope of looting the enemy's resources, but they were not obliged to abandon their farms. However, during full-scale foreign invasions or large expeditions of conquest, all able-bodied free individuals were obliged to fight. Celtic military organization was not so different from that of Feudal Europe, with an army being formed by several different contingents, each led by a noble warlord who commanded his own personal retainers. As we have seen, a certain number of the latter could be 'professional' fighters who earned a living as proper soldiers, but the majority were part-time warriors who had to serve in exchange for protection and benefits. Each warlord commanded a different number of warriors and there were no standard tactical units: a great noble could assemble thousands of men, while a minor one may lead into battle just a few hundred followers. The overall commander of a Celtic army, who could be a king or simply the most prominent warlord, usually experienced serious problems in keeping together so many ambitious military leaders and their warriors.

What we know for sure is that each tribal contingent was distinguished by its own insignia, which probably had a more symbolic function than actual tactical one. This general situation was even more difficult when a military expedition was organized having as its main objective the conquering and settling of new territories, in which case the warriors would have taken with them their families and all their goods (including animals). A Celtic campaign of conquest, as we will see, was a real mass migration that involved many thousands of individuals. On many occasions the Celtic tribes were 'peoples on the move', with the marching warriors being followed by the huge wagons of their families. Keeping order and some form of organization among this mass of people was extremely difficult, and something that only great military leaders were able to do. Unlike what happened during the previous 'Hallstatt' period, in the 'La Tène' period Celtic armies started to include a larger variety of troop types: while infantry remained the most important component from a numerical point of view, cavalry (formed by both chariots and horsemen) became increasingly decisive for the outcome of battles. The cavalry was entirely provided by the aristocracy, with warlords of superior rank mounted on chariots, while minor nobles fought as simple horsemen. As we will see, chariots could be used as mobile platforms during battles, but on numerous occasions they were simply employed to transport nobles on the battlefield. Nobles actually preferred to fight on foot when the enemy was deployed in close order. Chariots were effective as mobile platforms only when the battle was at its beginning (during the preliminary skirmishes from a distance) or when it was over (when the defeated enemy could be attacked from the rear, transforming the retreat

Celtic spearman with organic cuirass. (The *Ambiani*)

Celtic spearman with organic armour. (The *Ambiani*)

into a rout). All nobles, whether fighting on chariots or horses, had heavy personal equipment and wore full armour, and each of them was accompanied by one or more servants, driving the war chariot or taking care of the horse. Peasants/farmers would have formed the infantry, with the richest ones among them in the first lines, with their good personal equipment, while the poorest ones would have fought as missile troops with light infantry equipment. The bow was never very popular as a light infantry weapon among the Celts, as a result of which most of the skirmish troops were slingers and javelineers.

Celtic cavalry was excellent and proved superior if confronted by the mounted contingents deployed by Mediterranean armies. Celtic horses were not very tall or strong, but were generally bigger than those employed by the Greeks and Romans. In addition, Celtic horsemen were perfectly trained to charge enemy infantry by using their long slashing swords in a deadly way. With the exception of the Macedonian cavalry of Alexander the Great, the Greeks and Romans rarely used their cavalry as a 'shock' force to launch large charges. Instead, mounted troops were mostly employed for reconnaissance and auxiliary purposes. The Celts, however, gave great importance to the offensive capabilities of their cavalry and included large numbers of horsemen in their armies (up to one third of the total). The fact that cavalry numbers were so high can be explained quite simply: while nobles and professional fighters had war as their main occupation, the poorest individuals of the infantry were not obliged to serve on all occasions (as we have already seen). During their first encounters with Celtic cavalry, Mediterranean armies were shocked by their opponents: the Celts were better than any other European people at fighting on horse, with the only exception being those from the Eurasian steppes (such as the Scythians and Sarmatians). As time progressed, Celtic heavy cavalrymen became the most famous mercenaries of the Ancient World: they were employed by most of the Hellenistic armies (including that of Hannibal) and would later become the backbone of Rome's Imperial cavalry. Coordination between infantry and cavalry did not always work perfectly, especially because there were no good means to transmit signals or orders. Each tribal unit had its own musical instruments, but these were not used like those of the Roman legions, their only functions being to boost the morale of the troops and intimidate the enemy.

Chapter 3

The Celtic Conquest of Italy and the Sack of Rome

The first mass migration of Celts towards the plains of northern Italy took place around 600 BC, when the great warlord Bellovesus led a coalition of tribes across the Alps. The most important Celtic group marching towards Italy was the Senones, who were accompanied by several other minor tribes: the Aeduii, Ambarri, Arverni, Aulerci and Carnutes. The advance of the Senones initially encountered very little resistance and the newcomers were able to found several important settlements. During the following decades, the Celts who had settled in Lombardy continued the expansionist process initiated by Bellovesus and moved further south, soon reaching the Po River, around which some of the most fertile Italian plains were located. This region, however, was already inhabited by the Etruscans, who had built several important cities there, so the Celts were obliged to fight in order to continue their advance. The Senones were gradually joined by other important tribes, such as those of the Insubres, who founded an important new centre at Mediolanum (present-day Milan) from where to continue their advance. The Senones remained the main driving force of Celtic expansionism in Italy. According to Roman writers, they were the most violent and ferocious of all the Gauls. We know for sure that they continued to move south, defeating the Etruscans and other Italic peoples they found on their way (most notably the Umbrians and Picentes of central Italy). Before the Celtic invasions, the Etruscans were the most powerful people of Italy: their great cities dominated most of the peninsula and they had complete control over all trade routes. The city of Rome was ruled by a dynasty of Etruscan kings, while the Greek colonies of southern Italy had to fight with all their resources in order to stop Etruscan expansionism directed towards the south. The arrival of the Celts changed all this, the Etruscans having to abandon their expansionist ambitions in order to defend their home territories from Celtic incursions. The Etruscans fought more or less like the contemporary Greeks, with phalanxes of hoplites made up of heavy infantrymen, but their military formations had never faced an enemy as wild as the Gauls. By 400 BC, all the Etruscan cities of the Po Valley had fallen to the Celts, who had been able to advance further south, with the northern areas of central Italy located on the Adriatic coast occupied by the Senones, who had defeated the local Picentes.

In 390 BC, the Senones, guided by their great military leader Brennus, decided that the moment had come to move further south, with the objective of conquering the great

Celtic warrior with a fine example of leather cuirass. (The *Mediomatrici*)

Celtic warrior with organic armour. (The *Atrebates*)

Etruscan cities of Tuscany, as well as Rome. The first target of the new Celtic advance was the Etruscan centre of Clusum, at the time an ally of Rome. The Romans sent an embassy to Brennus to warn him that an attack against Clusum would be interpreted as a declaration of war against the Republic. During negotiations, however, a skirmish broke out between the Etruscan/Roman ambassadors and the Celtic representatives, during the clash one of the Senones was killed and the Gauls decided that the only action to take was to besiege Clusum. Since the Gallic warlord had been killed by one of the three Roman ambassadors, Brennus sent a delegation to Rome demanding they be handed over in order to obtain justice. The events happening in Clusum had given the Celtic leader a perfect *casus belli*, but the Romans responded to his requests by electing the three ambassadors as military tribunes with consular power. As a result, the Celts abandoned the siege of Clusum and marched south against Rome. The Romans knew practically nothing of the Celts and their battle tactics, having never fought a battle against them. At this time, Roman military forces were still organized according to contemporary Greek models and included a large phalanx comprised of the richest citizens. The Republic was able to assemble a large army of 35,000 men to face the Celtic menace, whereas Brennus commanded more or less 40,000 warriors. It is important to note, however, that only 24,000 of the Romans were well-trained legionaries, organized into four legions, while the remaining 11,000 soldiers were a hasty levy of untrained citizens. The decisive clash was fought on the Allia River, just a few miles north of Rome.

According to ancient sources, the Gauls of Brennus advanced much more rapidly than the Romans expected. The Romans had probably planned to fight the decisive battle on Etruscan territory, not just a few miles from their home. While the Romans mobilized their troops, Brennus was able to cover a great distance in just a few days. Having been surprised by the enemy, the Romans had no time to build their usual fortified camp and were not even able to divine the will of their gods before the battle (which was unacceptable for the deeply religious Romans). Being outnumbered by the enemies and knowing practically nothing of their tactics, the Romans decided to deploy all their forces in a very long single line in order to avoid any possible outflanking manoeuvre from the enemy, but this disposition made the Roman centre extremely thin. A number of Roman soldiers, possibly the badly trained reservists who had been hastily called up to serve, were put in reserve and placed on a hill located behind the Roman right wing. The Gauls launched a general and furious attack with all their forces along the whole line of battle. After a brief clash, during which the Roman soldiers could not manoeuvre due to their static formations, the Celts were able to break the enemy line at various points. The legionaries on the Roman left abandoned their positions and fled to the nearby Etruscan city of Veii, which had been

Celtic warrior with leather armour. (The *Atrebates*)

Celtic swordsman with organic cuirass. (The *Osismi*)

recently conquered by Rome, but their centre was annihilated by the Celtic charge. On the right, the Republican forces were able to maintain their positions a little longer thanks to the presence of the reserves on the hill, but eventually these soldiers were also obliged to fell back and retreated to Rome. Analysing the little information we have of the battle, it is clear that the Romans panicked as soon as the Celts launched their assault: these warriors from the north with their strange weapons and clothes, screaming like eagles and playing mysterious musical instruments, were terrible to the eyes of the Romans. Something similar happened when the soldiers of the Republic met with other 'beasts of war', the elephants of Pyrrhus, King of Epirus, a century later. Brennus and his warlords were surprised at how easy their victory had been: many thousands of Romans had been killed during the rout that followed the breaking of the Roman line, while Celtic losses were minimal. Rome no longer had a proper army and seemed ripe for conquest by the Gauls.

After despoiling their dead enemies, the warriors of Brennus marched towards the gates of Rome and were greatly surprised to find the city without defences. The gates were open and there were no soldiers guarding the walls, for the Romans had decided to defend only a portion of their city. Since there were not enough soldiers to guard all the walls, all the able-bodied men and political leaders had retreated to the Capitoline Hill. This strongly fortified citadel inside Rome, thanks to its position on higher ground, could be easily defended by a small band of men. All the weapons and provisions available in the city were massed on the Capitoline Hill, where the ruling families of Rome (those of the senators) had also found refuge. Most of the common people abandoned the city and fled to nearby centres that were allies of Rome. The 'Flamen Quirinalis' (the most important sacred symbol of Rome) and the Vestal Virgins who maintained it were also transferred to a nearby city. Many of the elder men, especially patricians and senators, decided to remain in the city and await the arrival of the enemy. Brennus led his men into the city and started to plunder all the houses. When the Celts reached the Forum, they found all the elderly patricians and senators waiting for them. The proud Roman aristocrats were immobile, to the point that the Gauls could not understand if they were real men or sculptures: very soon, however, the Celts realized that they were the aristocrats of Rome and killed them all. The plundering of the city was terrible, with all the houses destroyed by fire and most of the streets full of the bodies of inhabitants. Apparently the Celts decided to devastate the lower part of the city to break the morale of the defenders garrisoning the Capitoline Hill, but despite hearing the roaring of the flames and the screaming of the innocent victims, the soldiers guarding the citadel did not abandon their positions. After several days of sacking and killing, the Gauls realized that the defenders of the Capitoline had enough provisions to resist for a long period. As a result, Brennus decided to launch an attack against the citadel.

Celtic warlord with leather cuirass. (The *Mediomatrici*)

Common Celtic warrior with painted shield. (The *Trimatrici*)

The Celts, unlike the Greeks and Romans, were not experts in siege warfare. They were unable to build siege machines and usually only conquered enemy cities after the defenders had run out of provisions. In this case, however, Brennus could not wait that long, as the allies of Rome were already assembling military forces to confront the invaders and the Celts could have been trapped inside Rome while besieging the Capitoline Hill. The first assault of the Gauls was a failure: once the Celts were halfway up the hill, the defenders launched a deadly counter-attack that caused terrible losses to Brennus' warriors. After such a defeat, the Celtic warlord understood that it was impossible to conquer the Capitoline with frontal attacks. While these events took place inside the city, Brennus sent reconnaissance parties to the countryside surrounding Rome with orders to raid any kind of supplies that they could find. The devastated city simply could not feed the invaders for any length of time. During these raiding operations, the Celts were beaten by the allies of Rome, led by Marcus Furius Camillus (a great general of the Republic, who had abandoned Rome some years before due to personal issues). Soon after his victories, Camillus started to gather a new army, which also comprised the survivors of the River Allia who had fled to Veii. After hearing of the defeats suffered by his raiding forces, Brennus decided to launch a final attack against the citadel: this time, however, the Celts tried to reach the top of the Capitoline Hill by climbing it at night. The special operation was conducted by a small number of chosen warriors, all expert climbers. The Gauls were able to reach the top of the hill, but were said to have disturbed the sacred geese of Juno, which made such a noise that they alerted the Roman defenders, who repulsed the Gauls. While the famous episode of the Capitoline geese is obviously an invention, thanks to the ancient sources describing it we can plausibly suppose that the Gauls organized a night attack that was repulsed by the Romans.

During the following days, without any hope of conquering the enemy positions, the Gauls started to suffer from famine and pestilence. Brennus was still strongly determined to conquer the citadel, but his warlords were by now impatient to return home. As a result, the great leader was obliged to start negotiations with the Romans and the two sides agreed on a ransom of 1,000lb of gold. When the Romans delivered the gold, the Celts started to cheat with its weight: according to tradition, when the Romans protested, Brennus tossed his heavy sword on the scale with the famous expression *'Vae victis!'* ('Woe to the defeated!'). After being paid much more than the Romans had agreed, the Gauls abandoned the devastated city and went back to their territories in northern Italy. Brennus apparently understood that conquering and holding Rome was impossible, and thus what had started as a regular invasion had transformed into a raiding operation. Despite this, the Celts of Italy had obtained a magnificent victory. The Romans had been humiliated and lost most of their wealth; they never forgot this

Common Celtic spearman with painted shield. (The *Trimatrici*)

Celtic spearman with painted shield. (The *Trimatrici*)

great defeat of their early history, thereafter considering the Gauls as the most serious menace to their security. The sack of Rome initiated a new phase in relations between Celts and Romans, which would be marked by the implacable hatred of the latter for the heirs of Brennus. Despite the extent of such a military disaster, Rome only needed a few decades to fully recover, and the Republic never lost its expansionist ambitions and continued to exert dominance over central Italy during the following years. After securing complete dominance over the Etruscans, the Romans would soon start to move further north in order to once again face the Celts.

Chapter 4

The Celtic Expansion in Western and Eastern Europe

As pointed out in previous chapters, the great expansion of Celtic civilization across Europe was bolstered by the presence of a common 'pre-Celtic' culture in most territories of the continent. This was particularly true for the British Isles, where the arrival of the Celts did not mark a real revolution in the way of life. Since the Early Iron Age, both Britain and Ireland had been inhabited by peoples sharing many common features with the 'Hallstatt Culture'. In Britain the Iron Age began around 600 BC, more or less a century before in Ireland, and it was during this period that Celtic influence became increasingly stronger in the British Isles. The 'Celticization' of Britain was not characterized by mass migrations or violent campaigns of conquest. Although a good number of 'La Tène' Celts arrived in Britain from northern Gaul, these settled in a pacific way and soon mixed with the local populations (already organized in tribes). As time went by, especially during the fourth century BC, the whole population of Britain assumed the main characteristics of the Celtic 'La Tène Culture': the presence of the early immigrants from Gaul had been fundamental in this sense, since a quite limited number of settlers had been able to influence and change forever the civilization of the British Isles' original inhabitants. This process was a little slower in Ireland, Scotland and Wales, but provided more permanent results than in Britain. By the end of the fourth century BC, the whole of the British Isles had become home for hundreds of Celtic tribes, and only the territory of Gaul could be considered as more 'Celticized' than that of Britain. Slowly but steadily, the Celtic world had moved its core from the Alps to western Europe, a process that took place not only in Continental Europe, but also in the Mediterranean.

During the fourth century BC, some Celtic tribes started to move from southern Gaul and crossed the Pyrenees to enter Spain, which at the time was inhabited by the Iberians, a people with a high level of civilization and many cultural elements in common with the Celts. Differently from what happened in the British Isles, Celtic settlement in Iberia was characterized by frequent clashes with the local populations. The Iberians were strong warriors and their territory was rich in metals (fundamental for the production of weapons). As a result, the Celts were strongly limited by the resistance of the Iberians during their progressive advance in Spain. The Iberians, similarly to the Celts, were not a unified people, comprising several different tribes,

Celtic man wearing ordinary male dress. (The *Trimatrici*)

Celtic spearman with wicker shield. (The *Ambiani*)

controlling the whole territory of present-day Spain and Portugal. Since the foundation of Carthage, Iberia had been highly influenced by the Phoenicians, who controlled all the commercial routes passing along the coastline of southern and eastern Spain. As a result, Celtic penetration in Iberia proved to be easier in those areas of Spain and Portugal where the Carthaginian influence was still quite limited (and thus where there was a lower level of civilization). Around 300 BC, most of western and central Iberia had been occupied by the Celts, while the eastern part of the country was still inhabited only by native peoples. This situation remained unchanged until the Carthaginians conquered most of Iberia under Hamilcar Barca. In Gaul and Britain, the Celtic civilization was able to absorb that of the pre-Celtic peoples with no great difficulties, but in Spain, the Celtic and Iberian cultures mixed yet retained some of their most distinctive features. Thus, to indicate the Celtic tribes living in Iberia, scholars prefer to use the term 'Celtiberians', whose civilization was not fully Celtic and retained many elements of the previous Iberian culture. The term 'Celtiberians', however, was not invented in recent times, having been employed by ancient authors such as the first-century BC Greek historian Diodorus Siculus. This confirms that the 'hybrid' nature of the Celtiberians was already well known by other contemporary peoples.

During the fourth century BC, while the Celts from Gaul were expanding towards the British Isles and Iberia, those from Austria and western Hungary started to move across Eastern Europe. The main driving force of Celtic expansionism in this region was represented, at least initially, by the two large groups of the Boii and Volcae. These were not simply tribes, but confederations made up of several smaller tribal communities. Moving from Austria, the Celts completed their conquest of Hungary and advanced along the Danube in order to occupy large territories in the Carpathian region. During Antiquity, present-day Hungary was known as Pannonia, from the name of the most important people living in the area, the Pannonii, who were of Illyrian stock and thus had strong links with other Illyrian tribes living in the western Balkans. Similarly to what happened in Iberia, the Celts were gradually able to conquer most of Pannonia after experiencing frequent clashes with the local populations. By the end of this process, the Pannonians had acquired many distinctive Celtic features and thus the whole region could be considered as fully 'Celticized'. By the end of the fourth century BC, the Celtic presence in the present-day Czech Republic, Slovakia, Hungary and south-western Poland was quite stable, at which point the Celts decided to move further south and east, following two different routes. The first route crossed the territories of modern Slovenia and Croatia, in the northern part of the western Balkans, where the Celtic tribes had to face the Illyrians, who generally tried to resist with all their energies despite being outnumbered by the northern invaders. The second route followed the Danube and was directed to the Black Sea, running across

Common Celtic warrior. (The *Ambiani*)

Common Celtic infantryman. (The *Ambiani*)

Transylvania (the western part of modern Romania) and reaching the western part of present-day Ukraine. These areas of Eastern Europe were inhabited by the Dacians (a people of Thracian stock) and some fierce warrior peoples from the steppes of Eurasia (Scythians and Sarmatians). As we will see in the following chapters, the Dacians were gradually 'Celticized' due to the strong presence of Celtic tribes on the eastern borders of Transylvania, while in western Ukraine, cohabitation between the Celtic newcomers and the steppe peoples was much more difficult.

After having achieved prominence over various Illyrian tribes, the Celts arrived at the northern borders of the Kingdom of Macedonia, which under Philip II, father of Alexander the Great, had became the leading military power of the Greek world and was expanding across the Hellespont into the territories of the immense Persian Empire. For many years the Macedonians had been a sort of tribal kingdom with a mixed nature: their culture was Greek, but their way of life was similar to that of the Illyrian tribes settled on their northern borders. Philip II spent most of his life transforming Macedonia into a proper kingdom, with a modern army and stable institutions. He brought his country into the sphere of Greek civilization and subdued the Illyrians whose raids menaced the internal stability of Macedonia. When Philip II died, the throne was assumed by his ambitious son Alexander, who, before becoming the great conqueror of Asia, had to fight a series of campaigns against Balkan tribes during the early part of his reign. His enemies, the Illyrians and the Thracians, were also rivals of the Celts; as a result, there were no clashes between the Celtic tribes and the Macedonian forces of the young Alexander. At that time Alexander needed to secure his northern borders before moving against the Persians, as Macedonia had to be safe while most of the able-bodied men were far away fighting in Asia. The Macedonian monarch wanted to bring peace and order to all the Balkan lands located south of the Danube, which, in Alexander's vision, would have marked the border between the civilized world of the Greeks and the barbarian one of the northern tribes. During his northern campaigns, in 335 BC, Alexander was even able to cross the Danube at the head of an army, something that no other Greek military leader had ever done before. The Celts were particularly impressed by this and by the subsequent defeat of the Getae, a people of Thracian stock with many elements in common with the Dacians. After his victory over the Getae, Alexander decided to encamp near the Danube with his army, where he received embassies sent by all the peoples of the region, including that of the Celts. Each of the peoples submitted, at least formally, to the Macedonian king.

Thanks to Arrian, a formidable ancient source, we know some interesting details about the meeting between Alexander the Great and the Celt ambassadors which took place on the Danube in 335 BC. In the words of the Greek writer, the Celts were 'men

Celtic infantrymen in winter dress. (The *Ambiani*)

Celtic spearman with helmet and shield. (The *Teuta Arverni*)

of haughty demeanour and tall in proportion'; they came to the Macedonian camp with no intention to submit, but just to recognize Alexander as a capable military leader. The Celtic delegation wanted to offer their people's friendship to the foreign king and a proposal to reach a compromise that could be positive for both sides. The Balkan Celts wanted to avoid war with the Macedonians, but had no intention of discussing peace terms from an inferior position. Alexander obviously had different ideas, since he considered himself a true god and not a simple monarch. In order to test the temperament of the Celts, of whom he knew little, Alexander asked their representatives what they feared most in the world, expecting that the response would have been: 'You, great Alexander!' The Celts, instead, surprised him with an answer that perfectly reflected their mentality: 'We fear only that the sky fall and crush us or that the earth open and swallow us or that the sea rise and overwhelm us.' The Celts were saying that they feared nothing except the power of nature (which they respected as part of their religion). Alexander, initially infuriated by this response, soon understood that the Celts could have not answered any differently: they were a people of free and courageous warriors, the kind of men whom he had always admired all his life. As a result, a peace treaty was concluded between the Macedonians and Celts (which was positive for both sides). Alexander proclaimed himself a 'friend of the Celts' and promised that he would never invade their lands. Peace was maintained during his reign, but the situation on Macedonia's northern borders changed very rapidly after his death.

Around 320 BC, the Celts of the Balkans resumed their offensive attitude towards the southern territories occupied by the Illyrians. The Macedonian Empire was by now no longer in existence, being carved up in the outbreak of clashes between Alexander's successors. These generals had divided the former empire into many smaller kingdoms, which were constantly at war against each other. Macedonia, once the most powerful state of the Greek world, now had to fight against other kingdoms to maintain supremacy over the Aegean Sea. The Celts, soon understanding that this troubled situation could offer many advantages to them, moved against the Illyrians in the knowledge that the Macedonians would not support their adversaries. In 310 BC, the Celtic warlord Molistomos attacked deep into Illyrian territory, with the objective of defeating the main tribes living between Celtic territories and Macedonia. After a brief but extremely violent campaign, the Celts defeated and subdued three tribes: the Dardanians, Paeonians and Triballi. The Celts were now at the northern borders of Macedonia, whose ruler Cassander did nothing to stop them but simply offered refuge to the surviving Illyrians fleeing from the north. In 298 BC, the Celts attacked Macedonia and Thrace to raid their territories and possibly conquer some new lands. The Celtic advance followed two different directions: a first group entered

Celtic nobleman from southern Gaul armed with spear and shield; the practice of not wearing trousers was quite popular in the areas located around Massalia. (The *Teuta Arverni*)

Common Celtic warrior. (The *Ambiani*)

northern Macedonia, while a second one invaded Thrace. Cassander, at the head of the Macedonian military forces, stopped the first group and defeated it at the Battle of Mons Haemus, but the second group was able to advance through Thrace without encountering major opposition and defeated several of the local tribes. The victory of Cassander had saved Macedonia, but only for the moment, for the Celts had settled in Thrace, from where they could menace Greece and the rich territories of Asia Minor. Thrace was controlled by one of Alexander's successor generals, Lysimachus, who had been able to control the various Thracian tribes using very harsh methods, despite having an inferior military power compared with other successors like Cassander. In 281 BC, however, Lysimachus died in battle and his realm fell into a state of complete chaos, with various tribes revolting against the central authority. Meanwhile, Macedonia was also experiencing serious troubles, being ruled by a usurper king with very little military capability, Ptolemy Keraunos. Understanding that their moment had finally come, the Celts invaded Thrace and Macedonia in 279 BC.

Chapter 5

The Celtic 'Great Expedition' and the Birth of Galatia

In 280 BC, a large Celtic army left Pannonia and moved across the Balkans to invade Macedonia and Thrace. Comprised of 85,000 men, it was organized into three large columns. The first column, the most important one, moved against Macedonia and central Greece, while the second one attacked Thrace and the third was sent against the remaining Illyrians who still resisted. According to some ancient sources, this expedition was just a probing raid: the Celts were not ready to mount a full-scale invasion, but needed to test the enemy defences before moving with their families and goods in a mass migration. The division of their forces into three independent columns had negative consequences for the Celts. The first column, headed by the warlord Bolgios, was initially very successful but was defeated in a subsequent phase of the campaign. The Macedonians were surprised and defeated quite easily by Bolgios, with the Macedonian monarch, Ptolemy Keraunos, captured and killed by the Celts. Bolgios' warriors were apparently ready to invade Greece, but at this point they had to face the reorganized Macedonian military forces, now commanded by a much more experienced leader, a noble named Sosthenes. The Macedonians were able to defeat Bolgios, who was apparently satisfied with the treasures that his men had looted and thus ordered a general retreat of his forces. The column that attacked Thrace, led by Cerethrius, encountered fewer difficulties than Bolgios and returned home after having raided large areas of Thrace. The third column, guided by Brennus and Acichorius, easily defeated the Illyrians and then moved against Macedonia to support Bolgios. However, when Brennus and Acichorius arrived, Bolgios had already marched back to Pannonia. Despite this, the Celts decided to attack Sosthenes and his victorious army, practically destroying the Macedonians. Brennus and Acichorius were thus able to raid Macedonia against meagre opposition. However, after looting as much as they could, the Celts moved back north, realizing that they were too few to occupy Macedonia for a long time.

During 280 BC the Celts made the mistake of dividing their forces, and thus could not occupy and hold the lands that they had conquered and raided. However, they had been able to crush all the military forces sent against them and were now ready to advance again against Greece. Of the warlords taking part in the first expedition, Brennus had been the most successful. This historical figure, of whom we know very

Common Celtic infantryman. (The *Ambiani*)

Common Celtic spearman. (The *Ambiani*)

little, should not be confused with the other Brennus who sacked Rome a century or so before. Apparently, the name 'Brennus' meant 'someone outstanding' in the Celtic language, and thus was extremely popular among Celtic aristocrats. It could have been an honorific title, like the Latin word 'Magnus' ('Great'). Thanks to his great military capabilities, Brennus was chosen as the leader of a new expedition that the Celts of Pannonia decided to mount against Greece. This invasion, simply known as the 'Great Expedition' in Celtic history, took place in 279 BC. This time Brennus commanded a unified military force rather than an army divided in columns, and each warrior moving south also took with him his family and goods. According to ancient sources, the new Celtic invasion force comprised 176,000 men (152,000 warriors on foot and 24,000 on horse). While an impressive number, it should be noted that only 8,000 of the mounted warriors were proper cavalrymen, the remaining 16,000 being mounted servants who accompanied their masters on the field of battle and who could perform only auxiliary duties. There were two servants for each mounted noble warrior: the Greeks called this tactical formation used against them '*Trimarcisia*' (meaning 'Feat of three horsemen'). We don't know if the Celts also used this formation on other occasions, but each Celtic warlord fighting on horse was usually accompanied by a single mounted servant. It is possible that the expedition of Brennus could count on such a large number of slaves thanks to the high number of prisoners taken during the Balkan campaign of the previous year.

Since the Macedonian Army had been destroyed during the campaign of 280 BC, the Greek cities could no longer count on the military protection of their northern neighbours and thus had to assemble their forces in order to form a sizeable army. The Greek cities had always tended to be very suspicious of each other, forming large military alliances only in case of serious external threats: the Celtic menace was just such a threat considering the very high losses suffered by the Macedonians just a few months before. The cities of Greece were at that time among the richest in the world, with an unrivalled level of civilization, and could not accept being raided and looted by northern barbarians, or having to pay them to be left alone. As a result, the proud Greek communities temporarily forgot their internal divisions and assembled all their military forces to stop the invaders. The Athenians, Boeotians, Aetolians and Phocians all sent contingents to create a unified Greek army which was deployed at the mountain pass of Thermopylae, just north of Corinth. Once again, the destiny of the Greek world would be decided in that sacred and key position, as whoever controlled Thermopylae could control the whole of Greece. The Greeks had assembled an army of 24,000 infantry and 1,500 cavalry to stop Brennus: they were clearly outnumbered, but were sure that the terrain of the narrow Thermopylae pass would enable them to resist (as the Spartan-led Greeks had more or less two centuries before against the

Celtic warrior with painted shield. (The *Ambiani*)

Celtic infantryman with shield. (The *Ambiani*)

Celtic spearman with painted shield. (The *Ambiani*)

Persians). Brennus initially tried a frontal attack of the Greek defensive positions, but this was easily repulsed with severe losses for the Celts. The Celtic warlord understood that it was necessary to find an alternative solution. Most of his casualties had been killed by missile weapons and not during close combat with the Greek heavy infantry. The Greeks had deployed strong light infantry contingents on the slopes of the pass, which could easily harass the attacking Celts without risk, since they were located on higher ground. The Greek forces could additionally count on supporting fire from the Athenian fleet anchored near the Thermopylae pass.

In order to weaken the enemy defences, Brennus decided to send 40,000 of his infantrymen and 800 cavalrymen to pillage the territory of the Aetolians, who had sent one of the largest contingents of those defending Thermopylae. Brennus ordered his detached force to raid and pillage with great brutality to force the retreat of the Aetolians. His plan worked perfectly, as when the Aetolians heard that their home territory was menaced by the Celts, they soon abandoned the Greek positions. During the following weeks the Aetolians had to struggle for survival: being outnumbered, they defended their lands using guerrilla tactics, never facing the Celts in a pitched battle. After some initial difficulties, the tactics of the Aetolians proved very effective. Their homeland was entirely covered by mountains and hills, where their lightly armed infantry skirmishers could inflict heavy losses on the invaders without engaging in a proper battle. By the end of the Aetolian campaign, less than half of the original 40,000 Celtic warriors returned to join Brennus. While these events took place in Aetolia, the main Greek army experienced many difficulties, with Brennus able to outflank their defensive positions with another 40,000 warriors. According to contemporary sources, he used exactly the same pass that had already been employed by the Persians almost two centuries before. The Greek rearguard was completely surprised, the Celts attacking by charging out of the mist. Unlike the battle that resulted in the death of the Spartan king Leonidas and his force in 480 BC, however, this time the Greek rearguard was able to warn the rest of the army, which was able to escape from the trap. Although most of the Greek soldiers escaped, the army was disbanded, with each contingent returning to its home city, while the Celts occupied the pass. Greece was now open to attack, with no major forces to oppose Brennus.

After overrunning the Greek positions, the Celtic army continued to be divided, with the 40,000 warriors who had made the outflanking manoeuvre, under the command of Brennus, marching towards the treasure-filled sanctuary of Apollo at Delphi in Phokis, the most important religious site of the Greek world, famous for its oracle. Meanwhile, the larger part of the army, commanded by Acichorius, followed at some distance with the families and goods of the warriors. The forces of Brennus and Acichorius were harassed by large numbers of Greek skirmishers. The Greeks had learned that the

Common Celtic warrior. (The *Ambiani*)

Celts were unbeatable in close combat, thanks to their long slashing sword, and the only way to deter them was to fight from a distance, using missile weapons. Without proper knowledge of the territory, the Celts advanced slowly among the hills and mountains of central Greece, losing thousands of men without being able to fight a proper pitched battle. Before reaching Delphi, after also suffering from natural disasters like earthquakes and thunderstorms, the Celts were stopped by a Greek army made up of Aetolians and Lokrians. The Greeks had interpreted the natural disasters as the punishment of Apollo for the barbarians who wished to sack his sanctuary, and as a result found the courage to face the invaders on the battlefield. Meanwhile, the Athenians and Boeotians had rapidly reorganized their armies and were now ready to attack Brennus from the rear. During the ensuing clash, the advance of Brennus was soundly defeated by the Greeks, with the warlord being wounded. With the Athenians and Boeotians now behind them, the Celts had no choice but to regroup and retreat. Shortly after the battle, Brennus died from his wounds and Acichorius assumed overall command. The regrouped Celtic army retreated back to the Spercheios River, where it was ambushed and routed by a large Greek military force made up of Thessalians and Malians. The glorious 'Great Expedition', after having pillaged most of Greece, ended in failure: most of the Celtic warriors and their families were killed, with just a few being able to survive during the retreat, journeying to Thrace, where they settled in the Chersonese region. In 277 BC, however, the communities of Celtic refugees living in Thrace were also defeated by the new king of Macedonia, Antigonus Gonatas. After this latest disaster, the surviving Celts formed two groups: one abandoned the Chersonese and crossed the Hellespont to enter Asia Minor, while another smaller one decided to remain in Thrace and found a new city-state where the survivors could live and defend themselves. The latter was named Tylis and continued to exist for some time, until being finally destroyed by the Thracians in 212 BC. The defeat of the 'Great Expedition', however, did not mark the end of Celtic presence in the Balkans. The Boii, for example, continued to control most of Pannonia, while other tribes lived in stable settlements located in present-day Slovenia and Croatia. This situation changed only during the second half of the first century BC, when the Geto-Dacians of Romania organized themselves into a centralized kingdom under the guidance of their great leader Burebista, who stopped Celtic expansionism along the Danube and occupied most of the Carpathian basin (in present-day Transylvania).

The Celts moving to Asia Minor had better luck than those remaining in Thrace. They soon became known as Galatians, being the Greek equivalent of the Latin word for 'Gauls'. Apparently, the Celtic invaders came to Asia at the invitation of Nicomedes I, King of Bithynia, who wanted their military help in a dynastic struggle against his brother. Once in Anatolia, however, the Galatians did not respect pacts and started to raid the whole region. At that time, the dominant power in Asia Minor was represented by the Kingdom of Pergamon, ruled by the dynasty of the Attalids, who had become independent after the fall of Lysimachus' state (which had included Thrace and most of Anatolia). The Attalids had independently ruled the city of Pergamon since 281 BC; the founder of this new royal house had been Philetaerus, an officer of Lysimachus. The small military forces of the Kingdom of Pergamon, however, could not defeat the Galatians during their raids across Asia Minor. Over just a few years the Galatians became a serious menace for all the Hellenistic rulers of Anatolia, who were not strong enough to stop them. As a result, in 275 BC, the political stability of the region had to be re-established by a large Seleucid army from Syria commanded by Antiochus, the master of Asia. The Seleucids, who had the most powerful Hellenistic military force of the time, were able to crush the Galatians in 275 BC. After this defeat, the Celts of Asia Minor settled in central Anatolia, from where they continued to launch continuous raids against bordering lands. The Galatians settling in the centre of Anatolia belonged to three different tribes: the Tectosages, Trocmi and Tolistobogii. These settled on the plateau of Phrygia, after vanquishing the local inhabitants of Thracian descent, and this region, where the modern city of Ankara is located, soon started to be known as Galatia from the name of the newcomers. The three tribes organized themselves into a loose tribal federation, which exerted control over the subject Phrygian peasants. Originally, the Galatians in Anatolia could field a total of 10,000 warriors, which was later increased after the settlement became permanent. The Celts arrived in Anatolia with 160 war chariots of the conventional two–horse type used in Celtic Europe, but after settling on their new mountainous territory, the Galatians gradually abandoned the practice of using war chariots in battle. During the early phase of their settlement, the Galatians mostly supported themselves by plundering bordering countries or by serving as mercenaries in the various Hellenistic armies of the time. In 232 BC, the Attalids of Pergamon defeated them in battle, which eventually led to the creation of a reduced and more permanent Galatian settlement in central Anatolia that became a vassal of Pergamon. In 189 BC, after defeating the Seleucids at Magnesia, the Romans launched a large expedition against the Celts of Anatolia that became known as the Galatian War. After being defeated by the Romans, the Galatians lost much of their military power and were later invaded by Mithridates VI of Pontus. Thanks to the decisive help of the Romans, however, the Celts of Anatolia were able to regain their independence after the end of the Mithridatic Wars (88–63 BC) between Pontus and the Roman Republic. In 62 BC, Galatia formally became a client state of Rome and was officially organized as a kingdom; in 25 BC, this Kingdom of Galatia was finally annexed by the Roman Empire. From many points of view, Galatia can be considered as the only proper 'kingdom' created by the Celts during their expansion, and despite being isolated in the middle of the Hellenistic world, it played an important role in the history of Asia Minor.

Celtic warlord wearing ordinary male dress. (The *Trimatrici*)

Common Celtic infantryman. (The *Atrebates*)

After the 'Great Expedition' against Greece and their subsequent military exploits in Anatolia, the Celts started to be employed on a massive scale as mercenaries by the various Hellenistic states of the Greek world. The troops used by Antigonus Gonatas to defeat the Galatians were mostly composed of Greek mercenaries, who were extremely loyal to their leader. During the first years of his rule over Macedonia, Antigonus preferred to continue using Greek mercenaries and thus increased their numbers. In addition, he also recruited large numbers of Galatians as mercenaries and included them in his army, as after having been defeated, these fierce Celtic warriors were in search of employment. At a certain point, however, Antigonus Gonatas decided to reduce the number of Celts in his army and gave 5,000 of them to the King of Epirus, Pyrrhus, who had just returned from Italy after fighting against the Romans. By the end of Antigonus' reign, around 240 BC, recruitment of native Macedonians had again become very common and thus the use of Celtic warriors steadily diminished (their number never exceeded 2,000). After defeating them in Asia Minor, the Seleucids recruited a certain number of Galatians too. Firstly employed under Seleucus II (247-26 BC) after their settlement in central Anatolia, the Galatians fought in great numbers for Antiochus III at Magnesia (3,000 infantry and 2,500 cavalry). The peace treaty between the Seleucids and Rome, signed in 189 BC after the Battle of Magnesia, officially forbade the recruiting of troops west of the Taurus Mountains for the Seleucids, yet in spite of the treaty, the Hellenistic monarchs of Syria continued to use Galatian mercenaries in their army. Antiochus IV, for example, had 5,000 loyal Celtic warriors at his orders. The Seleucid lands located west of the Taurus Mountains were given by Rome to its Attalid allies of Pergamon, who as a result could start recruiting mercenaries from Galatia. In particular, once these Celts settled down in central Anatolia, the Attalids made use of their excellent light cavalry contingents.

Galatians were also employed as mercenaries in the Ptolemaic Army of Egypt and in the military forces of Herod the Great (ruler of Israel before its conquest by the Romans). Galatians started to be recruited in Egypt from 274 BC, but despite expectations, they proved to be undisciplined troops and never played a significant military role. Some of them were later transformed into 'military settlers' and remained in the country, but these were never a significant number. The Herodian Army included a large Royal Guard, which comprised about 2,000 Idumaeans, Thracians, Galatians and Germans (the last three groups being mercenaries). The Galatians serving Herod the Great had a very interesting history, as they had apparently been part of Cleopatra's Ptolemaic Army until 30 BC and were then assigned to Herod by Augustus as a reward for his loyalty. The Celts serving Cleopatra did not come from Galatia, but from Gaul; they were part of the 'Gabiniani', a Roman military contingent sent to Egypt during the dynastic struggles involving Ptolemy XII (the father of Cleopatra). Aulus Gabinius,

Common Celtic spearman. (The *Osismi*)

Celtic warrior with painted shield. (The *Osismi*)

the Roman proconsul of Syria, marched to Egypt at the head of a Roman provincial army and restored Ptolemy XII on his throne after a brief campaign. Before returning to Syria, however, Gabinius decided to leave 2,500 of his men at the orders of the restored king: the country was still on the verge of revolt and these Roman soldiers would have protected Ptolemy XII from any possible rebellion. Very soon, however, the Roman garrison of Egypt started to adopt the local manners and way of life, thus becoming completely alienated from the Roman Republic. After their integration into the Ptolemaic Army, these Roman soldiers transformed themselves into proper mercenaries and started to be known as 'Gabiniani' (from the name of their former commander). The 2,500 'Gabiniani' were not all Romans: 2,000 of them were proper Roman legionaries, while the remaining 500 were auxiliary cavalrymen from central Europe (Celts and Germans). Life in Alexandria was much better than the harsh Roman military discipline, as a result of which the 'Gabiniani' soon became the strongest supporters of the Ptolemies. Over time, they married local women and created new families in Egypt, and Ptolemy XII could always count on them, especially in case of internal revolts. When the king died in 51 BC, his oldest surviving children, Ptolemy XIII and Cleopatra VII, were supposed to rule jointly as husband and wife. Cleopatra, however, soon exiled her brother and started to rule alone, which put her in conflict with the 'Gabiniani', who later revolted and obliged Cleopatra to rule jointly with her brother, who returned from exile. In 49 BC, after the outbreak of the Roman civil war between Caesar and Pompey, the latter required military assistance from Egypt: Ptolemy and Cleopatra agreed to his requests and sent the 500 horsemen of the 'Gabiniani' to Pompey. A few of these, however, remained in Egypt at the service of Cleopatra and were later given to Herod after Augustus defeated the Ptolemies.

Galatian mercenaries were used also by the Kingdom of Pontus and the Bosporan Kingdom of Crimea. The army of Mithridates VI of Pontus was always a very multinational force. The ambitious king tried to develop a unified cultural identity among the different peoples living around the Black Sea region, in order to unite them against Rome and bind them to his personal power. In addition to his subjects, Mithridates could also count on several different sources of mercenaries/allies: Greeks, Thracians, Galatians, Scythians and Sarmatians. The Bosporan Kingdom was founded by Mithridates' son after his father's defeat, and the Bosporan military forces included Galatian and Paphlagonian mercenaries from Anatolia (who had previously served under Mithridates). Celtic mercenaries also became extremely popular in the western part of the Greek world, being employed on a large scale by the Sicilian city of Syracuse. The Syracusan Army was mostly formed by mercenaries during the whole Hellenistic period; Syracuse, thanks to its superior economic capabilities, was the only Greek colony in Sicily that could recruit and maintain an entire army of mercenaries.

Common Celtic swordsman. (The *Mediomatrici*)

Celtic infantryman with spear and shield. (The *Atrebates*)

The mercenaries serving Syracuse usually served in distinct units formed according to their nationality, being commanded by their own officers and equipped in their native style. At the time of the tyrant Agathokles (317–290 BC), the Syracusan Army included 1,000 Gallic mercenaries.

Chapter 6

The Fall of Cisalpine Gaul and the Invasion of the Cimbri and Teutones

After the sack of Rome, the Celts of northern Italy remained a formidable menace for the Republic for at least another century, the Gauls continuing to launch frequent and destructive raids against the territories of central and southern Italy. The Senones were the most active Celtic group taking part in this process, since they were settled on the territory of present-day Marche (an Italian region located in the middle of the peninsula and on the Adriatic coast). This area was still inhabited by the Picentes, who had been there for a long time until the arrival of the Celts. The Picentes had to submit because of the Senones' military superiority, but were always on the verge of open revolt. By this time the Celtic territories in northern Italy were already known as Cisalpine Gaul, the Romans using this expression to distinguish those lands from the Celtic territories in Gaul (which were collectively known as Transalpine Gaul). Rome, by now the dominant military power of central Italy, could not accept the Celtic presence in Marche or tolerate the frequent incursions launched by the Senones against the territories that were under its protection. As a result, as early as 360 BC, the Gauls and Romans went to war against each other once more. In that year, the Battle of the River Anio was fought between a Celtic raiding force and a Roman army. The Romans were able to prevail and completely annihilated the Gauls, also taking possession of all the goods that the Gauls had looted during their previous raiding expedition. This victory proved to the Romans that it was possible to defeat the Celts, and they realized that the Gallic menace had to be eliminated. After suffering other military defeats, the Celts of Cisalpine Gaul agreed to seek a peace treaty with the Roman Republic in 332 BC, according to which the Gauls were to retain all their territories in northern Italy, but would have to stop their raids against other Italian territories. The peace treaty was respected by both sides until 295 BC.

From 332–295 BC, the Romans, being secure on their northern borders, could launch new campaigns of conquest against the territories of southern Italy. These were mostly directed against the Samnites, the strongest people of that part of Italy. The Romans fought two wars against the Samnites without being able to defeat the southern warriors, who were masters in guerrilla operations but were also able to face a Republican army on the open field. A third war between the Romans and Samnites began in 298 BC,

Celtic spearman with painted shield. (The *Mediomatrici*)

Celtic warrior with spear and shield. (The *Mediomatrici*)

with the latter fighting for their survival. The conflict soon transformed itself from a local one into a 'national' war, gradually starting to involve most of the peoples living in the Italian peninsula. Those people were divided into two groups: one comprised Rome and all the peoples preferring the Republic's protection over freedom, the other comprising all those fearing the expansionism of Rome and desiring to remain free. It was a titanic clash of cultures, which culminated in the decisive Battle of Sentinum in 295 BC (also known as the Battle of the Nations). The Samnites were able to form a large military alliance against the Romans, containing the Etruscans, Umbrians (who had been partly 'Celticized' during the previous decades) and the Celtic tribes of Cisalpine Gaul. This confederation deployed a total of 60,000 warriors at Sentinum, the majority of whom were Samnites or Gauls. The Romans faced this 'multinational' army with just 38,000 soldiers, only receiving significant military support from the Picentes, who hoped that a Roman victory would expel the Celts from Marche. The Battle of the Nations ended in complete disaster for the confederates, with the Gauls, in particular, suffering the highest losses in the defeat. The Battle of Sentinum ended the third war between Romans and Samnites, resulting in the complete defeat of the Samnites, but also had important consequences for the Gauls, who had to abandon the territories of Marche. The territory was annexed by Rome and assumed the new denomination of Ager Gallicus, despite being formally given back to the Picentes, who had fought on Rome's side. In 283 BC, the Gauls tried to reconquer their former lands by forming a new alliance with the Etruscans, but they were again soundly defeated by the Romans.

In 249 BC, the Celts of Cisalpine Gaul, being in clear military difficulty, decided to ask for help against Rome from their 'cousins' of Transalpine Gaul. The Celts from present-day France, being in search of new lands to deal with overpopulation, gave a positive response to this request and sent a large army into northern Italy. According to ancient sources, this comprised 50,000 foot warriors and 25,000 on horse. Thanks to these new resources, the Italian Celts were able to resume hostilities against the Roman Republic. We have no precise details about these 75,000 warriors who marched south towards Italy: ancient writers call them 'Gaesatae', using a term that probably meant 'mercenaries' in the Celtic language. This seems to confirm that the 'Gaesatae' were not migrating to Italy with their families and goods, but were warriors who had been recruited by Cisalpine emissaries in the territories of Gaul. In those years the population of Transalpine Gaul was increasing quickly and there were too few resources to sustain such a large number of inhabitants. Minor warlords and young warriors were in search of new opportunities and new lands, because Gaul had little more to offer. The Cisalpine Gauls consequently had no problems in raising a large army of 75,000 mercenaries from north of the Alps. These warriors looked more 'barbarian' to the

Celtic foot warrior armed with spear. (The *Mediomatrici*)

Celtic spearman with painted shield.
(The *Mediomatrici*)

Romans than those living in northern Italy, having experienced very little contact with the Mediterranean world and thus having preserved their original Celtic identity. The Republic was surprised by the arrival of such a military force from Gaul, and initially had serious problems in containing the Celts. The new hostilities between Romans and Gauls lasted for many years, until 225 BC, the 'Gaesatae' proving to be excellent warriors and defeating the Republic on several occasions. In that year, however, a decisive clash was fought at Telamon between the Romans and Celtic military forces, and like at Sentinum seventy years before, the battle ended in complete disaster for the Gauls, who suffered enormous losses. The military potential of the 'Gaesatae' had been broken, but the same could not be said of the Cisalpine Gauls' spirit.

In 223 BC, in order to break the resistance of their enemy, the Romans sent an army of 40,000 soldiers to invade northern Italy. The Republic's offensive was very successful from the beginning, aided by some Celtic tribes deciding to side with Rome, hoping consequently to acquire new lands. During the following year, another large pitched battle between Romans and Gauls was fought at Clastidium, but yet again the Cisalpine Celts were defeated and their whole territory in northern Italy was occupied by Rome, including the important centre of Mediolanum. Cisalpine Gaul had fallen and the Romans were the new masters of the Italian peninsula. The Celts, however, had accepted surrender only because they had no more resources to continue the struggle. At the first occasion they would revolt again against Rome, in order to regain their freedom. In addition, it is important to note that the smaller Celtic communities living in the Italian Alps continued to fight against the Romans (albeit with guerrilla methods). These Alpine groups, settled in Italy for many years, had no intention of giving up their mountain passes. The Romans were still in the process of subduing them when a great foreign leader arrived to guide the Celts in their revenge: Hannibal Barca, the greatest warlord of Rome's bitter rival, Carthage. The Second Punic War between the Carthaginians and Romans broke out in 218 BC. Hannibal, after assuming command of the Carthaginian forces in Iberia, decided to march north and cross southern France in order to invade Italy over the Alps. This ambitious plan would have never been possible without the help of the Celts, as the Carthaginian army had to cross southern Gaul and use the Alpine passes controlled by the Cisalpine Celts. Like Alexander the Great several decades before, Hannibal proclaimed himself a friend of the Celts and soon became a leader to follow for most of the Gauls. In the years before the crossing of the Alps, Carthage had conquered most of Iberia, gaining the admiration of the local peoples (as we will see in the next chapter). As a result, the Punic Army included a large number of Celtiberians who were now serving as allies or mercenaries. The presence of these Celtic contingents helped Hannibal in gaining the support of the other Gauls he encountered during his march.

Modern reconstruction of a Celtic war chariot, of the same model employed against Julius Caesar in Britain. (Used by kind permission of Mike Loades)

Celtic spearmen with painted shields. (The *Mediomatrici*)

The Transalpine Gauls of southern France, fearing that the expansionism of Rome could also invest their lands, helped Hannibal by sending supplies and reinforcements, enabling the Carthaginians to reach the Alps without suffering significant losses. Rome was allied with the Greek colony of Massalia, but the latter was in no condition to stop Hannibal and his large army. During the difficult crossing of the Alps, most of the local Celtic tribes collaborated with Hannibal, although a few of them preferred attacking the Carthaginians with the hope of gaining some future reward from Rome. Despite many difficulties, Hannibal was able to guide most of his men across the great mountain range, and when he arrived on the plains of the Po Valley in northern Italy, thousands of Cisalpine Gauls joined the ranks of his army. As a result, the military forces commanded by Hannibal during his Italian campaign included a large number of Celtic warriors, be they Celtiberians, Transalpine Gauls or Cisalpine Gauls. Under the guidance of such a capable and intelligent military leader, the Celts fought magnificently on several occasions, making a telling contribution to all Hannibal's great victories on Italian soil. By 215 BC, it seemed that the Romans were no longer able to reconquer northern Italy from the Gauls, as Rome was menaced by the Carthaginians and all the Celtic peoples of Italy were now fighting on Hannibal's side. However, this situation soon changed and most of the Carthaginians were obliged to leave Italy in order to defend their home territories in Africa, which were invaded by a Roman army led by Scipio Africanus. Hannibal was decisively defeated by the Romans at the Battle of Zama in 202 BC, but this event did not lead to the surrender of the Italian Celts. Cisalpine Gauls had no intention of losing their new-found freedom, which had been obtained after many sacrifices. Aided by the presence of some Carthaginian troops still stationed on their territory, they decided to continue hostilities against Rome. In 200 BC, at the Battle of Cremona, the Celts and their Carthaginian and Ligurian allies were defeated by the Romans. This clash proved decisive for the destiny of Cisalpine Gaul, and although the campaign continued until 194 BC, the Celts were by now no longer strong enough to contest Roman dominance over their lands in northern Italy.

The second century BC marked the beginning of the end for the Celts of Gaul, with the southern part of present-day France conquered by the Romans. In addition, that period of Celtic history was characterized by the terrible invasions of Germanic tribes, notably those of the Cimbri and Teutones. By the end of the Second Punic War, the Romans had almost completed their occupation of both northern Italy and Iberia; the territories of southern Gaul were located between these and were crossed by the only land route connecting Italy with Iberia. As a result, they were an obvious target for Roman expansionism. The Romans had not forgotten the help given to Hannibal by the local Celtic tribes, and with the support of their Greek allies from Massalia, they soon occupied the region of Provence. Before describing these events, however, it is helpful to look at what had happened in the Celtic territories located north of the Alps. As we have seen, Austria and Switzerland had been the core regions of the early Celtic civilization, and by the second century BC, despite becoming more marginal in the Celtic world, had developed some distinct local features. Austria, by now called Noricum by the Romans, had seen the creation of a confederation of tribes, with the various independent Celtic communities living in Austria and Slovenia gradually unified in a sort of 'federal' state. This Kingdom of Noricum did not have the same stable organization as the Kingdom of Galatia created by the Celts in Asia, but it could be compared with the latter in many aspects. The Celts of Noricum had strong political and commercial relations with those living in Pannonia and the other Celtic tribes settled in Switzerland. Noricum was also in a delicate geographical position, with Roman Italy to the south and the fierce Germanic peoples to the north. The Kingdom of Noricum was created around 150 BC, and from the start the rulers of this confederation maintained very good political relationships with the Romans, providing them with large amounts of excellent weapons in exchange for military protection. Noricum was famous for the high quality production of metal weapons and tools. The ancient territory of Austria was rich in iron, gold and salt, which both the Romans and the Germans badly needed, and thus the Celts of Noricum had to maintain some kind of equilibrium in order to preserve their independence. Noric steel was particularly appreciated for its quality and hardness: most of the Roman weapons produced from the times of the mid-Republic were made with metal coming from Noricum. The Celts of Austria remained loyal allies of Rome for many years, benefiting from the fact that the Republic needed a 'buffer zone' on its northern borders. In Switzerland, the situation was similar to Austria, but the local Celts had a less positive relationship with Rome. By the second century BC, the Swiss plateau was entirely occupied by the Helvetii, who lived on a territory that was full of natural resources and especially of gold, which could easily be found in many rivers as well as in mines. The Helvetii were not a single tribe, but a confederation of four tribes: from an organizational point of view, their community was similar to the Celtic one existing in Noricum. Apparently, the Helvetii originally lived in southern Germany, but around 150 BC, under strong pressure from Germanic tribes, they had to move south and settle in the Alpine area. It is tempting to assume that both the confederation of the Helvetii and the Kingdom of Noricum were formed around the middle of the second century BC as a result of Germanic mass-migration. These movements of the Germanic tribes culminated just a few decades later with the spectacular invasions by the Cimbri and Teutones.

After the end of the Second Punic War, the Greek colony of Massalia continued to be a loyal ally of Rome and started to experience some serious difficulties in containing the incursions of the Celtic tribes living in southern France. The Gauls, however,

Celtic standard–bearer, warlord and spearman (from left to right). (The *Mediomatrici*)

Celtic heavy cavalryman in full equipment, with helmet and chainmail. (*With thanks to John Conyard, www.comitatus.net*)

were not the only menace for Massalia: the Ligurians, who lived on a tract of Gaul's Mediterranean coast, also caused serious trouble for the security of the Greek city. Ligurian pirates frequently assaulted the merchant ships arriving at or departing from Massalia, making the vital trade routes of the city extremely dangerous. In 181 BC, at the request of Massalia, the Romans sent military forces to destroy the Ligurian pirates: the Republic had strong interests in that area of the Mediterranean, especially after the conquest of Sardinia and Corsica, which were occupied following the end of the First Punic War. In 154 BC, the Romans mounted another expedition against the Ligurian tribes of southern France, again in collaboration with their allies of Massalia. This time the defeat of the pirates was decisive, and the Greek colony could resume control over the area's commercial routes. During the following decades, however, the region of southern Gaul continued to experience internal tensions, the Celts starting to augment their pressure on Massalia by launching more frequent and more destructive raids. By 125 BC, a confederation of various tribes, collectively known as the Salyens, threatened the city of Massalia. At this point the Romans decided to intervene: their first objective was to save their Greek allies, but they already had in mind to expel the Celts from most of southern Gaul. After two years of harsh campaign, the Roman military forces destroyed the Salyens and their capital. The newly conquered territories were not given to Massalia, but were annexed by the Republic (the Romans even founded a colony on the former homeland of the Salyens, which would later be known as Aix-en-Provence). In 122 BC, the remaining forces of the Salyens revolted against Rome and were joined by other major Celtic tribes from other areas of Gaul, the Arverni and the Allobroges. During 122-21 BC, the Romans had to use large military resources to subdue the Celts of southern France, who surrendered only after being defeated in two large pitched battles which caused them enormous losses. After these victories, the Romans annexed all the Celtic lands located between Iberia and northern Italy, with only Massalia remaining formally independent, albeit being practically surrounded by Roman territories. The territories of Rome in southern Gaul soon became known as Provence, since they were organized as one of the Republic's provinces. A few years after these events, however, Roman dominance over southern Gaul was shattered by the arrival of ferocious Germanic tribes, the Cimbri and Teutones.

The Cimbri and Teutones were from the Jutland peninsula, in present-day Denmark, southern Scandinavia being inhabited by many different Germanic tribes in the second half of the second century BC. In those years there was a demographic explosion in the region, which obliged many of the local tribes to migrate south in search of new lands with enough natural resources. The Cimbri and Teutones, moving together, crossed the territories of eastern Germany and reached Pannonia, where, after some bloody battles with the Celtic Boii, they were repulsed. At this point the

Celtic javelineer with oval shield. (The *Teuta Arverni*)

two tribes turned west and invaded the Kingdom of Noricum, but the Romans were rapid in helping their Celtic allies and sent a large army to Austria to repulse the invaders. The combined military forces of Rome and Noricum faced the Cimbri and Teutones at the Battle of Noreia in 112 BC, but the clash was a disaster for the Romans, who suffered severe losses without being able to stop the Germanic advance. At this point, after having devastated Noricum, the Cimbri and Teutones could have easily crossed the Alps and invaded Italy, but instead, they decided to cross Switzerland and

Celtic light skirmisher with javelins. (The *Atrebates*)

attack southern Gaul. In 111 BC, the Germanic invaders entered the territory of the Helvetii, who instead of fighting against the newcomers, decided to join the Cimbri and Teutones in their invasion of Roman Provence. Apparently, however, not all four tribes of the Helvetii joined the Germanic raiders. In 109 BC, the Cimbri and Teutones obtained a first victory over Roman military forces in southern France, followed by another at the Battle of Burdigala in 107 BC. Two years later, at the Battle of Arausio, the Romans suffered another terrible defeat: 80,000 legionaries were killed by the Germanic warriors in one of the Republic's worst military disasters. The Cimbri and Teutones seemed impossible to stop, the two peoples on the move comprising an impressive total of 200,000 warriors with their families and goods. They were desperate and had nothing to lose: they needed new land on which to settle and were willing to do everything possible to reach their objective. The Germanic warriors fought with a fury that had never been seen before by the Romans, to whom they looked like wild barbarians because they had a primitive culture if compared with the Celts of earlier times. Fearing that the Cimbri and Teutones could now move south and devastate Italy, the Romans decided to elect as supreme commander their best general, Gaius Marius.

Luckily for the Romans, during 104-03 BC, the Cimbri and Teutones moved to the north of Iberia after crossing the Pyrenees, where they pillaged and destroyed all the settlements that they found on their way, meeting no resistance. Their raids made no distinctions: the central and eastern areas under Roman control were pillaged, as well as the western ones that were still independent and inhabited by Celtiberian tribes. In 103 BC, however, the Celtiberians organized a large coalition comprising most of their tribes and faced the invaders on the open field, and for the first time in many years, the Germanic raiders were defeated and obliged to abandon Spain. The two years spent in Iberia by the Cimbri and Teutones were fundamental for the Romans, giving them enough time to gather an impressive number of fresh military forces. In addition, during those two years, Gaius Marius completely reorganized the Roman Army and transformed it into a highly professional force. In 102 BC, the Cimbri and Teutones marched back across southern Gaul, with the clear intention of crossing the Alps to invade Italy, but this time they made the fatal mistake of dividing their forces. Gaius Marius was waiting for them, defeating the Teutones first at the Battle of Aquae Sextiae (Aix-en-Provence), where he killed over 90,000 of them. The Roman victory was followed by the complete extermination of the Germanic tribe: the warriors' families were massacred or captured and all their goods were pillaged. While Gaius Marius was fighting against the Teutones, the Cimbri were able to cross the Alps and penetrate into Italy. Their advance, however, was extremely slow, which gave Gaius Marius the time to return and give battle. At the Battle of Vercellae, in 101 BC, the ferocious Cimbri were also completely annihilated by the new Roman army of Marius:

Celtic javelineer with light equipment. (The *Ambiani*)

120,000 Germanic warriors were killed or captured, together with their families. Gaius Marius had wiped out two entire peoples with just two bloody battles: the hegemony of Rome over Provence was restored, and central and northern Gaul were now also open to Roman expansionism. The Celtic world was about to change forever.

Celtic slinger with light equipment. (The *Atrebates*)

Chapter 7

The Roman Conquest of Iberia and Gaul

A ncient Iberia was inhabited by two main ethnic groups: in the west and the centre of the peninsula there were the fierce communities of Celtiberians, while in the east there were the powerful Iberian tribes. Since 575 BC the Carthaginians had started to create commercial colonies on the southern and eastern coast of Spain, but these exerted only a limited influence over the local populations. This situation changed completely with the outbreak of the Punic Wars: Carthage, unlike Rome, could count on few human and natural resources because the territory of North Africa was not as rich as that of Italy. As a result, the Carthaginians badly needed new territories from which they could take natural resources (for example minerals or metals) and recruit large numbers of good soldiers. Iberia was their natural choice: ancient Spain was extremely rich in mineral resources, especially gold and silver, while the local tribes were well known in the Mediterranean world for the deadly skills of their warriors. Iberian slingers from the Balearic Islands, for example, served as mercenaries in most armies of the time and were considered as an elite force by the military leaders who employed them. The Iberians, similarly to the Celts, produced magnificent weapons which were exported through the entire Mediterranean world and influenced the combat techniques of both the Carthaginians and Romans. Two weapons, in particular, became iconic of the Iberian warriors: the *falcata* (a sword with a single-edged blade that pitches forward towards the point) and the *gladius* (a short stabbing sword, used to strike with the point). The latter became the standard weapon of the Roman infantry, being adopted by the legions after the Republic fought against the Iberians. Spanish armies of the time included excellent contingents of heavy infantry and cavalry, but also deadly light skirmishers. The Carthaginians understood that by using such a great military potential they would be able to face the Roman legions. As a result, after defeat in the First Punic War, Carthage sent its best general – Hamilcar Barca, father of Hannibal – to conquer Iberia. After eight years of campaign, masterfully using both force of arms and diplomacy, Hamilcar was able to take most of central and eastern Iberia. The local tribes accepted Carthaginian supremacy, but in most cases retained a high degree of autonomy: the Carthaginians had permission to exploit the natural resources of the territory, but could not interfere with internal politics. In case of war, the Iberians were to provide large military contingents to

Celtic standard-bearer with parade helmet. (G.A.S.A.C.)

Celtic standard-bearer with light equipment. (The *Ambiani*)

Carthage, which could be made up of allies or mercenaries, and would form the largest part of Carthage's army. Hamilcar died while crossing a river, before he could conquer the western territories of the Celtiberians. However, when his son Hannibal assumed command of the Punic Army, the Iberians were already extremely loyal to Carthage's cause and ready to fight against Rome.

During the Second Punic War, understanding that Carthage's power was based on the resources of Iberia, the Romans sent various generals and armies to Spain to expel the Carthaginians from the area. After several bloody battles, by the end of the conflict, the Romans were able to conquer and occupy all the Iberian lands that had been under Carthaginian control. The local tribes, however, continued to revolt against the Republic for many decades, for while Punic control had not been very strict, Rome's rule was completely different. During these rebellions the Iberians were helped by the Celtiberians of western Spain, who had remained independent from both Carthage and Rome. As a result, the Romans soon understood that the only way to pacify Spain was to also conquer Celtiberian territory. This, however, proved extremely difficult. Celtiberians were masters of guerrilla warfare and had a perfect knowledge of their mountainous territory. The first Roman military operations against the Celtiberians started as early as 197 BC, just a few years after the end of the Second Punic War. From the beginning, military operations in Spain were characterized by a series of crushing defeats for the Romans. In 181 BC, the first of two Celtiberian Wars broke out in Spain, ending in 179 BC when Tiberius Gracchus signed peace treaties with most of the Celtiberian leaders. The Romans had not been able to subdue Celtiberian lands,and thus the peace treaties were quite favourable for the Celts of Spain. They retained complete control over their lands, but in exchange had to provide allied military contingents and amounts of grain to Rome. In 154 BC, after several decades of relative peace in Iberia, the Second Celtiberian War started. This conflict lasted for two years and included a series of great Celtiberian victories. In order to prevail, the Romans had to use very harsh methods, fighting with great violence and committing a series of abuses against the civilian population. By 151 BC it seemed that the Celtiberians had finally been defeated by Rome, albeit they were still in control of most of their lands. Since 155 BC, however, the Iberian tribes of southern Spain had launched a general revolt against the Romans. This was guided by the great military leader Viriathus and became known as the Lusitanian War (from the name of Viriathus' tribe, the driving force of the rebellion). In 144 BC, the Celtiberians decided to break their pacts with Rome and joined Viriathus in his revolt, uniting most of the Iberian and Celtiberian tribes for the first time in pursuit of a common objective. Viriathus' dream was to expel the Romans from all Iberian territories. His war lasted for more than 15 years, ending only in 139 BC. During the Lusitanian War the Romans were on the verge

Celtic standard-bearer with spear. (The *Ambiani*)

Celtic heavy infantryman (left) and standard-bearer (right). (The *Ambiani*)

of losing Spain on several occasions, but finally Viriathus was assassinated and the rebels crushed. After these events Iberia became Roman Hispania and the Republic's dominance over most of present-day Spain/Portugal became much more stable. Most of the Celtiberian lands were occupied, with the exception of some small territories located in north-western Spain, where, in present-day Cantabria and Asturias, two tribes continued to resist using irregular warfare tactics. The area was extremely marginal from an economic point of view, being entirely covered with mountains and located on the western edge of Roman-held territory, as a result of which the Cantabri and Astures were able to retain their independence until the reign of Augustus, aided by the fact that after the invasions by the Cimbri and Teutones the Romans were mostly occupied with their bloody civil wars. After becoming the sole master of Rome and its first emperor, in 29 BC, Augustus finally launched a campaign of conquest against the Cantabri and Astures. This ended only after ten years of harsh fighting, during which the Imperial armies experienced many difficulties. Cantabria and Asturias were among the last Celtic lands to fall under Roman dominance.

Gaul, the core of Celtic civilization in Europe, was conquered in a very short time compared with Iberia. Unlike what happened in Spain, the Celts living in present-day France had to face a single but incredibly effective Roman commander: Julius Caesar. He started to rule Rome jointly with Crassus and Pompey from 60 BC, when the three formed the First Triumvirate. In 58 BC, after being consul in Rome for one year, Caesar obtained the proconsulship of Cisalpine Gaul (northern Italy) and Transalpine Gaul (southern France), and the great general and future absolute ruler of the Republic badly needed a major military victory in order to consolidate his power and limit the ascendancy of his two colleagues/rivals. Crassus was the richest man in Rome and had already obtained a great military triumph during the slave revolt of Spartacus, while Pompey had conducted and won many brilliant campaigns against the toughest enemies of Rome. Caesar was ambitious and had great personal capabilities, but unlike the other members of the Triumvirate he had never been at the head of a large army. Obtaining command over the troops of the two Gauls was a great opportunity for Caesar: those provinces were 'border' areas at the time, where a young and intelligent general could learn a lot by fighting against local enemies. The vast adjacent Celtic lands of central and northern Gaul were waiting for Caesar and his legions. Caesar knew very well that by conquering Gaul the Republic would become the greatest power of the time, for with the natural resources and population of Gaul at their disposal, the Romans could have conquered Continental Europe. Caesar had four veteran legions at his command and was ready to start his campaign of conquest: he only needed a *casus belli* to justify the outbreak of hostilities in the eyes of the Senate. This was given to him by the Helvetii, who were experiencing increasing pressure from the Germanic tribes living on their northern borders and were planning to migrate across the territories of Rome in search of a new land.

The Helvetii wanted to settle on the Atlantic coast of central Gaul and hoped to do so without having to fight during their journey, but to reach their objective they had

Celtic standard-bearer with chainmail. (*Antichi Popoli/Confraternita del Leone*)

Celtic standard-bearer with 'Ciumesti' helmet. (*Antichi Popoli / Confraternita del Leone*)

to cross Roman Provence and the territories of the Aedui (another Celtic tribe, the most important ally of the Romans among the Gauls). Caesar was extremely cunning in using this situation to his advantage, presenting the migration of the Helvetii as an invasion in order to force the Senate's hand and obtain permission to face this menace with his military forces. When the Helvetii started their march, only one of Caesar's four legions was stationed in Transalpine Gaul. Being in no condition to mount an offensive, he initially tried to gain some time through peace talks with the emissaries of the Helvetii. The Celts wanted to negotiate a safe and peaceful passage across Roman territories, having no intentions of raiding or pillaging the areas that they were going to cross. After holding talks for two weeks, during which he fortified his positions and levied more troops, Caesar refused all the requests of the Celtic emissaries. At this point the Helvetii tried to enter Roman territory, but were easily repulsed by the new defences organized by Caesar. Meanwhile, Caesar went to Cisalpine Gaul to raise two new legions and bring all his military forces north of the Alps. Knowing full well that they were now going to face all of Caesar's military potential, the Helvetii initiated negotiations with the Sequani and Aedui to form a military alliance against Rome. The Sequani accepted and allowed the Helvetii to cross their lands without opposition, but the Aedui remained loyal to Rome and had their lands devastated by the migrating Helvetii. Responding to Aedui requests for help, Caesar attacked the Helvetii with three legions while they were crossing the Arar River. When the Romans arrived, three of the four Helvetian tribes had already crossed the river and Caesar was only able to destroy the remaining one. Caesar, however, continued his close pursuit with great determination. During the ensuing Battle of Bibracte, fought in 58 BC, the Roman legions were finally able to crush the Helvetii, who suffered enormous human losses, and the few survivors surrendered to Caesar and were sent back to their home territories, where they were to continue to live in peace as subjects of Rome.

Victory over the Helvetii, however, did not end hostilities in Gaul, with the Sequani and Aedui continuing to fight each other after their territories were freed from the Helvetii. These two tribes, probably the most important ones of Gaul, had been at war for a long time and were divided by a very deep rivalry. The Aedui had become loyal allies of Rome mostly due to their frequent wars with the Sequani, since they needed a powerful ally to prevail over their rivals. In 63 BC, however, the Sequani had found a strong ally in the Germanic tribe of the Suebi. Guided by the great warlord Ariovistus, the Suebi had joined their military forces with those of the Sequani in exchange for lands in Gaul. At the Battle of Magetobriga (63 BC), an alliance formed by the Sequani, Arverni and Suebi had soundly defeated the Aedui, which had caused great apprehension in Rome, where memories of the devastations caused by the Cimbri and Teutones were still alive. The presence of the Suebi in Gaul was considered a real menace, and the

Republic had the clear intention of breaking the alliance between Ariovistus and the Celtic tribes. After the joint military operations against the Helvetii, the leaders of the Aedui manifested to Julius Caesar their concerns about Ariovistus' expansionism. The Aedui formally asked for Roman military help to defeat the Suebi and their Celtic allies, provising the occasion that Caesar was waiting for to continue his campaigns in Gaul. The Roman general sent an ultimatum to Ariovistus, warning him that no Germanic warrior could cross the Rhine without causing a reaction by Rome. When some Celtic allies of the Suebi attacked the Aedui, Caesar had no choice but to strike at Ariovistus. In the ensuing Battle of Vesontio (58 BC), the Suebi were comprehensively defeated, losing thousands of men, and the few survivors were obliged to cross back over the Rhine in order to save their lives. Another quarrel between Celtic tribes in 57 BC gave Caesar the opportunity to start a new campaign. This time the menace for Rome's Gallic allies was represented by the Belgae, a powerful confederation of Celtic tribes living in the northern part of Gaul (in present-day Belgium).

The Belgae were extremely strong from a military point of view and had experienced very little contact with the Mediterranean world, instead being heavily influenced by the Germanic tribes living on the other side of the Rhine. The Belgae 'confederation' had been formed during 58 BC in order to balance Caesar's increasing political influence over Gaul, but this had been interpreted as a menace by the Aedui and the other local allies of Rome, who feared that such a powerful confederation could conquer most of Gaul. Caesar's military operations against the Belgae proved extremely difficult, and the Romans were nearly defeated at the Battle of the Sabis (57 BC), which proved to be decisive for the destiny of the Belgae as after the clash, Caesar was able to conquer most of the enemy settlements and gradually crushed the resistance of the Belgae, who had lost most of their best warriors during the battle. By the end of the year, all the territories of the Belgae were in Roman hands, after which it became clear to Caesar's Celtic allies, such as the Aedui, that the Romans were gradually conquering the whole of Gaul by using the internal divisions of the Celts. In 56 BC, Caesar moved against the Celts of Armorica, who lived on the northern Atlantic coast of Gaul and had formed a tribal confederation following the example of the Belgae with the hope that this could stop Roman expansionism. The territories of the Armorican Celts included Brittany and Normandy, and thus were strongly linked to the Celtic communities in Britain. In addition, the Armorican 'confederation' included the important tribe of the Veneti, the only Celtic community to have seafaring capabilities and a fleet of warships. The campaign against the Veneti proved very difficult for Caesar, who had to build a fleet on the English Channel and fight with all his resources, both on land and at sea. Thanks to an intelligent use of innovative amphibious tactics, the Romans were finally able to prevail over the Armorican Celts and defeated them on the difficult terrain of Normandy.

Celtic standard-bearer with crested helmet. (*Antichi Popoli/Confraternita del Leone*)

Celtic warrior with carnyx. (The *Trimatrici*)

Caesar used 55 BC to mount two punitive expeditions on the borders of Gaul, one against the Germans and the other against the Britons. After the defeat of Ariovistus and his Suebi, other Germanic tribes living to the east of the Rhine had continued to mount frequent raids against Gaul. In order to show his Celtic allies that he was still the protector of Gaul, Caesar organized a punitive campaign against the Germans, crossing the Rhine to punish the raiders on their own territories. Both the Germans and Celts were highly impressed by Caesar's subsequent actions, as the Romans built a massive bridge over the Rhine and crossed the river with large military forces. No other military leader, Roman or Celtic, had achieved anything similar, and the Germanic tribes were taken by surprise and defeated quite easily. After this victory Caesar turned against the Britons, in order to punish them for the support given to the Celts of Armorica during the previous year. The Romans disembarked in southern England with two legions, but this time Caesar's campaign was a failure, bad weather destroying a large part of the Roman fleet while the landings were opposed very effectively by the Britons, who employed war chariots on a large scale, which the Romans were not prepared to face. Caesar returned to Britain at the head of a larger military force in 54 BC, having this time made all the necessary preparations to face the Britons on equal terms. The Catuvellauni, the most important Celtic tribe in southern England, were defeated and obliged to pay a yearly tribute to Rome. Caesar's expeditions in Britain had not given new territories to Rome, but were extremely important for the propaganda of the general: no other Roman military commander had ever moved so far north, reaching what were the edges of the known world. Julius Caesar was at the peak of his personal power, but the tribes of Gaul were now on the verge of revolt. Having seen the fall of the Helvetii, Belgae and Armoricans, it was by now clear that Caesar wanted to be the sole ruler of Gaul and thus the only way to stop him was to form a 'national' confederation of Celts that would fight to oust the Roman presence. Some Gallic leaders started to understand that unity was a key factor: the Celtic tribes had been defeated by Caesar because they had fought with no coordination and some important groups, such as the Aedui, had preferred to help the invaders with the objective of obtaining political advantages.

A true sense of 'Gallic identity' had gradually developed, especially following the most recent campaigns of Caesar. In 54 BC, the Eburones of northern Gaul revolted against the Romans. Having previously been vassals of the Belgae, but now under the guidance of their charismatic leader Ambiorix, they mounted a full-scale rebellion against Rome. Julius Caesar had sent a total of 9,000 men to garrison the territory of the Eburones, but these were mostly inexperienced levies without previous combat experience. As a result, when the revolt of Ambiorix began, they were easily defeated by the Eburones and expelled from their territory. At this point the Eburones tried to

Detail of a carnyx. (The *Trimatrici*)

raise a general revolt of all the Belgae, but the arrival of Caesar with a large number of troops prevented them from achieving their objective. In 53 BC, after several months of harsh fighting, 50,000 well-trained Romans were finally able to crush the Eburones and their allies, including some Germanic tribes. Northern Gaul was brought back under Roman control, albeit with many difficulties, but meanwhile the most powerful Celtic tribes in the centre of the country were assembling all their forces under the leadership of the greatest Gallic warlord of all times, Vercingetorix. He had become 'king' of the Arverni thanks to popular support, after defeating the faction of his own tribe that wanted to maintain peace with the Romans. Vercingetorix's charismatic leadership was able to unite all the tribes of central Gaul against Rome, he founded a new Gallic capital at Gergovia and was able to obtain support from all the social groups of Gaul. Before him, only the aristocrats of the various tribes had been determined to fight against the Romans: the common peasants and farmers had never been particularly enthusiastic to risk their lives against Caesar's legionaries. Vercingetorix proposed a new vision to the whole Celtic world, comprising a much more democratic approach

Celtic warrior with carnyx. (The *Ambiani*)

Celtic warrior with crested helmet and carnyx. (*Antichi Popoli / Confraternita del Leone*)

Celtic warriors playing nice examples of carnyx. (*Antichi Popoli / Confraternita del Leone*)

to political questions, which gave him the complete support of the lower social classes and enabled him to raise very large military forces.

Vercingetorix became supreme commander of all Celtic military forces in 53 BC, when for the first time in Gallic history he imposed strict discipline and secured for himself the loyalty of all the tribes by taking hostages. Instead of fighting against Caesar in a pitched battle, he preferred defending some key locations of his territories by fully exploiting the natural fortifications provided by the terrain. The great Gallic warlord undertook a scorched earth strategy, which included burning villages and fields to prevent the Romans from living off the land. This caused some discontent among the Celts but also enormous logistical difficulties to Caesar, who soon ran out of supplies and was obliged to provoke the enemy in order to fight a decisive battle as soon as possible. This clash finally took place at Gergovia, Vercingetorix's capital, where the Celts were able to prevail and for the first time defeated the Romans in a great battle. However, they suffered high losses and were unable to pursue Caesar effectively. Both sides needed time to reorganize their forces; Vercingetorix, in particular, was awaiting the arrival of massive reinforcements from other areas of Gaul. As a result, he decided to retreat to the most important Gallic stronghold, Alesia, a fortified city that was considered unconquerable by most contemporary observers. After reorganizing his forces, Caesar marched to besiege Alesia and built a first wall around the city to isolate the defenders from the outside world. After some time, however, 100,000 Celtic warriors reached Alesia to reinforce Vercingetorix's forces and Caesar risked being trapped between two large Gallic armies, one surrounding his forces and the other stationed in Alesia. Caesar then ordered the construction of a second wall to protect his legions from the assaults of the Celtic reinforcements. The joint attacks of the Gauls, mounted from inside as well as from outside, very nearly achieved victory. The Roman defences were almost broken and only a desperate counter-attack launched by Caesar with his last reserves saved the legions from total defeat. After the failure of these assaults, the reinforcements were routed and abandoned Vercingetorix to his destiny. The Gallic leader finally surrendered after having run out of supplies, following an incredible but hopeless resistance. Alesia was conquered by Caesar in 52 BC: Gaul had fallen, after centuries of Celtic prosperity. However, the dramatic struggle between Celts and Romans was still far from being ended.

Chapter 8

The Decline of the Eastern Celts
and the Conquest of Britain

Celtic settlements in Eastern Europe had always been less stable compared with those in the western part of the continent, but had proved to be fundamental for the cultural development of the areas where they were located. By 60 BC, before Caesar initiated his conquest of Gaul, the situation of the Celtic communities in modern Eastern Europe was as follows: in Anatolia the Kingdom of Galatia continued to exist, albeit smaller and as a vassal of Rome (the Kingdom of Pergamon had been annexed by Rome since 129 BC); in Macedonia and Thrace all the Celtic settlements had long before been destroyed by Antigonus Gonatas; in Transylvania the Celts were facing increasing pressure from the Thracian kingdom of the Getae and Dacians (who had joined forces to form a unified state); in western Ukraine the local Celtic communities, after having mixed with the Scythians for some time, had been gradually pushed out by the arrival of new invaders from the steppes (most notably the Sarmatians, who had also wiped out the Scythians); in south-western Poland, the Czech Republic and Slovakia the Celts came under increasing pressure from the Germanic peoples, who were migrating west marching along the Danube; Pannonia was still the most important Celtic area in the region, but by now no longer had expansionist ambitions; and Noricum was still formally independent, albeit having become a vassal of Rome after the invasion of the Cimbri and Teutones. This general situation completely changed in a few decades as a result of the great political events taking place during the following period.

The Kingdom of Galatia, after being ruled by puppet monarchs from 62–25 BC, was finally annexed to the Roman Empire by Augustus after the fall of Egypt and the death of Mark Antony (Galatia had been one of the client states supporting Mark Antony and Egypt in the struggle against Augustus). Since 62 BC, Galatia had deployed a regular army organized according to contemporary Roman models and trained by Roman military officers. Deiotarus, who was made King of Galatia in 62 BC as a reward for the military support given to Pompey, restructured the military forces of his realm as thirty *cohortes* (the equivalent of three Roman legions) and levied a total of 14,000 soldiers (12,000 infantry and 2,000 cavalry). These took part in the wars against Mithridates of Pontus as loyal allies of Rome, but after some severe defeats

Celtic warrior with crested helmet and decorated horn. (*Antichi Popoli/Confraternita del Leone*)

Example of Celtic decorated horn. (*Antichi Popoli / Confraternita del Leone*)

had to be reduced to a single legion. This force, however, continued to fight on the side of the Romans during Caesar's brief campaign against Pontus in 47 BC. After the death of Caesar, the Galatians made a crucial mistake: they decided to side with Mark Antony and thus lost their independence after he was defeated in 30 BC. With Galatia's incorporation into the Roman Empire, the single legion of the kingdom was absorbed into the Roman Army, whicgh at the time already included twenty-one legions, so the Galatian one became known as *Legio XXII Deiotariana* (from the name of the king who had founded it).

The Kingdom of Noricum, located in present-day Austria and Slovenia, had a very similar destiny to that of Galatia. The local Celtic tribes had joined Caesar in his struggle against Pompey in 48 BC, but in 16 BC made the mistake of joining forces with the Pannonian Celts to invade Roman possessions in the northern Balkans. As a result, that same year, Augustus sent an army against Noricum, which was annexed into the Roman Empire. The military forces of Noricum, still organized according to Celtic tribal models, were absorbed into the Roman Army to form some auxiliary units (which were stationed on the Alps). Massalia, which had remained the only city of Gaul independent from Roman rule, was also annexed by the Romans at this time. During the civil war between Caesar and Pompey, the Greek colony had decided to side with Pompey. In 49 BC, the military forces of Caesar destroyed the fleet of Massalia and occupied the city, thus ending its long history of alliance with Rome.

The Celts of Transylvania were annihilated by Burebista, who formed a unified kingdom in present-day Romania after assuming control over the many Thracian tribes living in this large region of Eastern Europe. The Thracians of Romania could be divided into two groups: the Dacians and the Getae. While the former were prominent from a numerical point of view, the latter were extremely powerful militarily because of the strong influence exerted over their warriors by the military traditions of the steppe peoples. Burebista, after becoming king in 60 BC, was able to cancel the traditional rivalries existing between the Dacians and Getae, and formed an impressive army by mixing the best elements of the two groups. As we have seen, Celtic tribes had long before settled in Transylvania (the western part of modern Romania) and had gradually started to exert a strong influence over the Dacians. As a result, by the time of Burebista, the Dacians had been strongly 'Celticized', unlike the Getae, who had little contact with the Celts). Around 150 BC, however, this peaceful mix of cultures came to an end, the Dacians started to show Celtic economic and cultural expansionism, organizing themselves into a proper kingdom. This process reached its highest point with the ascendancy of Burebista to the Dacian throne: he first extended dominance of the Dacians over the territories of the Getae before moving against the Celts in order to expel them from Romania. Burebista was a great military leader and had a large number of troops under his command, so it was not particularly difficult for him to defeat the Celts, notably the Boii, who were forced to abandon Transylvania and had to move west, resettling in the Celtic territories of the present-day Czech Republic. The tribe of the Taurisci was also defeated by Burebista and had to resettle in present-day Slovakia. By 50 BC, after more or less ten years of campaigns, the Celtic presence in Transylvania had been completely destroyed. Burebista continued his expansionist policy by conquering the Greek colonies located on the eastern shores of his new kingdom, and by 45 BC he had completed the unification of Romania in a single and extremely powerful Dacian kingdom. During the civil war between Caesar and Pompey, the ambitious monarch sided with the latter, to the irritation of Caesar. Both Burebista and Caesar were assassinated in 44 BC, and thus a conflict between Rome and Dacia was avoided (at least for the moment). The centralized kingdom created by Burebista did not survive after the death of its founder, being replaced by four smaller Dacian 'states'.

The Boii and Taurisci, after moving respectively to Bohemia (Czech Republic) and Moravia (Slovakia), enjoyed several decades of peace, but soon had to face a new and much more deadly menace: the Germanic tribes of the Marcomanni and Quadi, who were migrating across central Europe in search of new lands where to live. During this time most of the Germanic tribes had abandoned their original settlements in Scandinavia and northern Germany and were now on the move. Their large population needed space and abundant natural resources to survive, something that they could not find in their original homelands. The Marcomanni and Quadi invaded the Celtic territories of Bohemia and Moravia around 10 AD, the former defeating the Boii, while the latter crushed the Taurisci. As a result, Bohemia and Moravia became part of the expanding Germanic world, while the Celtic settlements in south-western Poland were also conquered by the Germans around this time. Maroboduo, King of the Marcomanni, created a powerful confederation of Germanic tribes in the area previously inhabited by the Celts, which represented a terrible menace for the Roman Empire during the next two centuries. While these events took place in the north, Pannonia fell under Roman control, thus practically ending Celtic presence in Eastern Europe. Most of Pannonia, as we have seen, was occupied by Celtic tribes, yet these had mixed with the local Illyrian communities and thus gradually created a sort of 'multicultural' country. Celtic tribes lived in the northern part of Pannonia, along the Danube, while Illyrian ones inhabited the southern areas, maintaining strong contacts with the other Illyrians of the western Balkans. Rome fought three wars against the Illyrians during the period 230-168 BC, which ended with the complete annihilation of most of the Illyrian tribes, apart from those living in Pannonia, who remained independent.

Example of Celtic ordinary horn. (The *Trimatrici*)

After the death of Julius Caesar, the Illyrians, hoping to gain some advantages from the chaotic political situation of Rome, rose up in open revolt and defeated the Roman garrisons operating on their territory. For some years they were able to regain their former independence, until being crushed by Augustus during a series of harsh campaigns fought in 35–33 BC. During these military operations the Illyrians of Pannonia supported their southern 'cousins', and consequently Augustus mounted a first Roman raid into Pannonia and occupied some southern territories of the region. During 17–16 BC, the Celts of Noricum and Pannonia launched an invasion of the Roman province of Macedonia, but were promptly defeated and repulsed, this campaign ending with the fall of Noricum. The northern part of Pannonia, however, remained independent after these campaigns. In 14 BC, the Illyrians of southern Pannonia rebelled against Roman rule, with the help of the Celts living in the northern part of the country. The new war lasted until 9 BC and the Roman reconquest of southern Pannonia; in addition, some northern territories of the Celts were occupied by the legions. It was by now clear that Roman predominance in the region was becoming absolute, and the only chance for the Celts and Illyrians to survive was to unite themselves against the common menace and regain some form of independence. After some years of relative peace, the

Celtic 'Hallstatt' cuirass with geometrical decorations. (*G.A.S.A.C.*)

Celtic warlord with 'Agen-Port' helmet. (The *Ambiani*)

Celts of Pannonia and all the Illyrians (those from both southern Pannonia and the western Balkans) revolted against Augustus in AD 6. The ensuing campaigns, lasting for three years, proved extremely difficult for the Romans, who were defeated on several occasions. In the end, thanks to their superior military capabilities, the Romans were able to prevail and annexed to the Empire the last independent lands of northern Pannonia. Initially the territory corresponding to present-day Hungary was annexed to the large province of Illyricum, which had been created in 168 BC with the lands conquered from the Illyrians. In AD 14, however, the province of Illyricum was divided in two in order to have a better system of defence: the original territories of Illyricum were reorganized into the new province of Dalmatia (roughly corresponding to the lands of ex-Yugoslavia), while Pannonia was organized as an independent province.

Celtic standard-bearer with 'Agen-Port' helmet. (The *Trimatrici*)

By AD 10, there were no more independent Celtic communities in Eastern Europe: the glorious days of the Galatians had come to an end.

Around AD 40, only the Celts of Britain and Ireland remained independent from Rome. Thanks to their relative geographical isolation, they had been able to preserve their identity from the great political and cultural changes taking place in Europe at the time. From 50 BC to AD 40, the Romans had to consolidate their conquest of Gaul and faced a series of small revolts in the region which were suppressed with no particular problems. The Celtic warriors from Gaul soon started to be employed by the Romans as auxiliaries, particularly in the cavalry, being greatly appreciated for their courage and superior weapons, as well as for their horses. Caesar already employed large numbers of allied Gallic heavy cavalrymen: he even sent 1,000 of these to his ally Crassus, for the campaign against the Parthians that culminated in the catastrophic Roman defeat at Carrhae (where these early Gallic auxiliaries were all killed in the Mesopotamian desert). Once the Empire was consolidated in Continental Europe, the Romans could seriously start planning an invasion of Britain. Following Caesar's expeditions, the Celts of southern Britain had continued to send tributes and hostages to Rome in order to retain their independence, but from the time of Augustus it became clear that the Romans would invade the island at the first opportunity. In AD 43, the Roman emperor Claudius finally ordered the invasion of Britain, which was conducted by an army of 40,000 men, half of whom were professional soldiers from four different legions. The early resistance of the Britons was guided by the Catuvellauni, a powerful confederation of tribes that had already fought against Julius Caesar. The decisive battle of this first phase of the campaign was fought at the River Medway in Kent, where the Celts assembled their forces to stop the Roman crossing. After two days of fighting, during which they came very near to defeat, the Roman legions were finally able to prevail. After this victory the Romans had to accomplish the difficult crossing of the Thames and thus fight another battle, but the Catuvellauni were defeated again and their capital of Camulodunum (modern Colchester) was occupied.

By the end of the AD 43 campaign, the Romans controlled most of south-eastern Britain. In the following years, until AD 60, the legions also conquered south-western Britain and started to move north. The Romans encountered the strongest resistance in Cornwall and Wales; the latter, in particular, proved extremely difficult to occupy due to the hills that covered most of the territory. The Celtic tribes of Wales defended their territory using guerrilla methods instead of facing the Romans in open battle. By AD 60, however, most of Wales had been conquered, but the outbreak of Boudicca's revolt prevented the legions from creating stable military settlements in the region. Boudicca was queen of the Iceni, one of the most important Celtic tribes in south-eastern Britain. These had already fought against Rome in AD 47 and had been soundly defeated, but the Romans permitted them to retain some degree of autonomy. With

Nice example of 'Agen-Port' helmet. (The *Mediomatrici*)

Nice example of 'Agen' helmet. (The *Trimatrici*)

the ascendancy of Boudicca, the Iceni took advantage of the Romans' heavy military involvement in Wales to launch a general rebellion. Boudica may be seen as the female equivalent of Vercingetorix: thanks to her great charisma, she was able to unite most of the Celtic tribes in Britain against the Romans. The revolt clearly showed that the

Roman presence in Britain was not yet well consolidated, with the druids still the real masters of the territory. Most of the tribes had formally submitted only to gain enough time to reorganize their forces. Initially Boudicca's army was victorious on various occasions: the rebels took and destroyed the city of Camulodunum, wiped out an entire Roman legion sent against them and even occupied the new Roman settlement of Londinium (the future city of London, founded around AD 45). After these initial but serious defeats, the Romans were able to reorganize their military forces in Britain and faced Boudicca's large army at the Battle of Watling Street, which ended in complete disaster for the Celts, who suffered enormous losses. After this defeat the revolt was easily crushed by the Romans and Boudicca committed suicide.

The years between AD 60 and 78 saw the Romans complete their conquest of Wales and expand their territories towards northern Britain. Agricola arrived in Britain as the new Roman governor of the island in AD 78. An experienced military commander, his main objective was to expand Rome's territories towards Scotland. After first defeating the last independent tribes of northern England, such as the Brigantes, he moved across southern Scotland, earning brilliant victories over the local Celtic communities. Scotland, known as Caledonia by the Romans, was inhabited by some of the wildest tribes ever encountered by Rome. They had experienced very little contact with other civilizations and were thus much more difficult to conquer than the tribes of southern Britain. Thanks to an intelligent use of amphibious tactics, Agricola was able to subdue most of Caledonia in just a few years: in AD 83-84 he even reached Aberdeenshire and the Scottish shores of the North Sea, where he defeated a large army of Caledonians (who had formed a confederation against him) at the Battle of Mons Graupius. When recalled to Rome in AD 84, Agricola left most of Scotland in Roman hands, with only the territories in the extreme north-west of Caledonia remaining independent. After the departure of Agricola, the succeeding Roman governors of Britain did little to consolidate the conquest of Caledonia. Fortifications built in the region were abandoned, while most of the local tribes rapidly regained their autonomy. The Romans gradually retreated to the border between northern England and southern Scotland, where a stable *limes* (boundary) was established in AD 122 with the construction of Hadrian's Wall. During the period AD 122-42, the Romans attempted to reoccupy at least the Scottish Lowlands, but encountered strong resistance from the Caledonians. Realizing that it was impossible to move further north into the Scottish Highlands, the Romans established a new *limes* in AD 142 by building the Antonine Wall in order to divide the Lowlands from the Highlands. Despite these efforts, the Romans were forced to abandon the Lowlands of Caledonia in AD 162 and retreated south to Hadrian's Wall. During the following decades the Romans made at least four significant attempts to reconquer Scotland, but all were repulsed by the Caledonians, the most important being made by Septimius Severus in AD 209. Scotland and Ireland would remain Celtic to this day.

Celtic warrior with 'Port' helmet. (The *Mediomatrici*)

Example of Celtic painted shield. (The *Mediomatrici*)

Chapter 9

Celtic Arms and Armour from the La Tène Period

With the development of the new 'La Tène' cultural phase and the contemporary expansion across Europe, the panoply of Celtic warriors started to be much more varied and complex than before. Developing much more frequent and stable contacts with other peoples, the Celts began to adopt military elements that were characteristic of other civilizations, while at the same time starting to influence the military models of those fighting against them. Generally speaking, Celtic arms and armour did not change dramatically during the long La Tène Period, yet by analyzing surviving artefacts, it is clear that there was a slow but steady evolution. Of all the components that made up the panoply of a Celtic warrior, the helmet was probably the most peculiar: unlike other pieces of equipment, helmets could vary greatly since several different models were in use at the same time. At the beginning of the La Tène Period, Celtic helmets could be of three different kinds: hemispherical, conical or of the so-called Negau type. Hemispherical helmets were extremely simple: they were produced from a single piece of bronze and were plain, having only a simple ridge around the base. Conical helmets were much taller and could frequently have a quite impressive steep apex, which could be surmounted by decorative feathers of various colours. This kind of protection for the head was much more costly and difficult to produce than the simple hemispherical helmet; in addition, conical helmets were frequently decorated with rich incisions on their external surface. These two elements, together with the frequent presence of decorative feathers, could suggest that conical helmets were mostly produced for noble/rich warriors while the hemispherical ones were the standard issue for common warriors. In later periods, the hemispherical helmet would develop into the new 'Coolus' model, while the conical headwear was progressively abandoned. The hemispherical helmets gradually started to have a larger protective ridge on the back, which later expanded to become a proper neck guard (the latter being the main feature of the new 'Coolus' model). Conical helmets like those employed during the early La Tène Period were also used by other peoples of the time, such as the Veneti in Italy, as their shape was perfect to avoid serious injury caused by blows coming from above.

Apparently there were also some helmets mixing features from the hemispherical and conical models, such as the famous 'Agris Helmet' found in central France and dating

Example of Celtic oval shield. (The *Mediomatrici*)

Examples of Celtic painted shields. (The *Mediomatrici*)

back to 350 BC. This parade helmet was entirely covered by gold foil on its external surface and decorated with a series of rich sculpted motifs connected with pieces of coral. The 'Agris Helmet' is vaguely conical in shape, but has a small neck guard similar to the later hemispherical helmets. It is a unique example in the production of Celtic helmets for its quality, having surely belonged to an extremely rich and important warlord. Negau helmets were a direct evolution of the previous double ridge helmet or 'Buckelhelm', consisting of a pot-shaped lower part having a wider brim around its base. The previous transversal ridges, surmounted by a large crest made of horsehair, were initially reduced in their dimensions and later completely substituted by a single ridge (this no longer being topped off by a crest). Negau helmets generally had few decorations, so we can suppose that they were also used by common warriors as well as nobles. This kind of protection for the head was extremely popular in the Balkans, but also in Italy, being employed on a large scale by important groups such as the Illyrians. During the middle La Tène Period, these three basic models of helmet started to be supplemented by others, which are collectively known as parade helmets: these were not employed in battle and had only a ceremonial function. Generally speaking, they had more or less the same shape of the hemispherical or conical helmets, but were characterized by the presence of rich decorative elements. These could consist of horns (in various different shapes) or could reproduce in a stylized way the general appearance of sacred animals. These decorations were placed on the peak of the helmet and were quite impressive, especially if the general shape of the helmet was conical. A perfect example of these parade helmets is the so-called 'Waterloo Helmet' found in the Thames and dating back to 150 BC, which has a hemispherical shape but is characterized by two conical horns with terminal knobs. Another famous Celtic helmet having decorative horns is the *Elmo di Casaselvatica*, of the later 'Montefortino' model, but with two massive horns riveted on its two sides. This kind of horned helmet was probably also employed by the Ligurians, on whose territory the *Elmo di Casaselvatica* was found.

Around 300 BC, Celtic helmets started to assume their definitive conformation, with the progressive abandonment of previous models and the creation of four new ones: 'Montefortino', 'Coolus', 'Agen' and 'Port' helmets. The Montefortino soon became the most popular of the four, being used on a massive scale by Celtic warriors. It was so effective and easy to produce that it was later also adopted by the Romans, who transformed it (with a few adjustments) into the standard helmet of their legions. Its name derives from the Italian place where the first helmet of this kind was discovered. The Montefortino has a round shape with a raised central knob and a protruding neck guard; the former was usually surmounted by coloured plumes, while the latter was generally decorated with incisions. In addition, unlike previous Celtic helmets, the Montefortino has a pair of cheek pieces, which could be of two main different kinds, according to their shape. The first model of cheek pieces reproduced the stylized shape of the check, while the second was trilobate, consisting of three little discs having the shape of a triangle. Trilobate cheek pieces were apparently influenced by contemporary helmets and armour of the Italic peoples, which frequently included this peculiar combination of three discs, but over time this kind of cheek pieces was abandoned and the other became dominant (being the one adopted by the Romans). In general terms, Montefortino helmets had many positive features: they were easy to produce, gave excellent protection to the wearer's face, could be easily decorated in many different ways and were comfortable enough to be worn for a long time. All these characteristics made the Montefortino the most popular helmet of the Celtic world. It could be decorated in numerous ways in order to transform a simple helmet into a parade one. As we have already seen, decorative horns could be applied on its external surface (like for the *Elmo di Casaselvatica*), while the basic central knob could also be substituted with a central insert with several branches and hollow finials (on which

Some products of the Celtic blacksmiths. (The *Trimatrici*)

multiple feathers could be applied). But decorations could be even more complex, like in the case of the famous 'Ciumesti Helmet' found in Romania: this has a bronze spike instead of the central knob, on which there is a fixed cylinder sustaining a massive decorative bird. We don't know if the latter is a raven, an eagle or a falcon: all three birds were sacred according to Celtic religion. The eyes of the bird are made of yellow ivory and have a red enamel pupil, while the wings are impressive for their large dimensions and are applied to the main body of the bird in a very peculiar way: as a result, when the wearer of the helmet is running, the wings go up–and–down, simulating the flight of a real bird and producing a terrible metallic noise (a sort of psychological weapon). Other sacred animals of the Celts that were reproduced on parade helmets included boars, deer, wolves, foxes, bears, horses and bulls.

The Coolus helmet co-existed for a long time with the Montefortino, being later adopted by the Romans on a large scale. It had a simple round shape, with a ridge running around its base, and on the back this ridge enlarged to become a sort of neck guard, similar to that of the Montefortino. In addition, the Coolus helmet had a couple

Some products of the Celtic blacksmiths. (The *Trimatrici*)

of cheek pieces that reproduced in a stylized way the human cheek. Being extremely easy and cheap to produce, the Coolus helmet became very popular, especially with the auxiliaries of the Roman Army. According to archaeological finds, cheek pieces were only added to Coolus helmets at a later date, as a result of the Montefortino's influence. Therefore, at least initially, the Coolus helmet looked more or less like a simple metal cap. Crest fittings were only added at a later date by the Romans. The Agen helmet is characterized by a wide brim at the lower edge and looks more or less like a bowler hat, with a general shape that is hemispherical and a prominent ridge between the main body of the helmet and the brim. Agen helmets did not initially have cheek pieces, but later adopted those attached to Coolus ones. Unlike the latter, Agen helmets had plumes on a central knob. The characteristic brim was narrow at the front of the helmet and wide at the back, while in the central part of the helmet's length the brim was reinforced by a V-shaped section, apparently derived from the peculiar brim of the Boeotian helmets used in the Hellenistic world. The Port helmet was quite similar to the Montefortino, being round in shape and having a ridge running around its base which, on the back, expanded to become a proper neck guard and was reinforced by two smaller ridges. On the front, this kind of helmet was characterized by the presence of embossed eyebrow decorations, which had a very practical function in helping to deflect blows. Cheek pieces were of the same kind applied to Coolus and

Agen helmets, and there was no central nob for sustaining plumes. During the Roman period, the Agen and Port helmets mixed some of their main characteristics and gave birth to the famous 'Imperial-Gallic' family of helmets.

In recent years, the various aspects related to Celtic armour have been widely discussed by scholars in order to find a response to the many questions we still have regarding it. Did the Celts use body armour on a large scale? Did they use leather armour or only bronze cuirasses and chainmail? Was armour used only by rich/noble warriors or also by common soldiers? Finding a definitive response to these three basic questions is not easy. First of all, we should describe the Celtic concept of 'heroic nudity', which was different from that of the Greeks. Many Greek/Roman authors and artists have described or reproduced Celtic warriors as naked fighters, attacking their enemies with no personal protection and being equipped only with their offensive weapons. Whether this general picture can be applied to all Celtic warriors or only a specific number of them can probably be found in some peculiar aspects of Celtic religion. A true warrior, in order to show his personal valour, would have marched into battle without armour and armed only with his sword, demonstrating his total faith in the gods and his contempt for death. As a result, we could plausibly suppose that the presence of naked warriors in Celtic armies was probably due to some specific religious practice that was used to show a fighter's courage and religious zeal. Maybe it was a sort of initiation rite for younger warriors or a religious practice performed by a 'brotherhood' of warriors who had dedicated their lives to the gods. From ancient sources, for example, we know that the Gaesatae frequently fought naked: maybe this was linked to the peculiar condition of mercenaries, who had dedicated their entire life to war? What we do know for sure is that Greek and Roman writers/artists emphasized the presence of naked warriors in Celtic armies in order to present the Gauls as wild barbarians with a lower level of civilization. It was a propaganda operation, clearly visible in some important artistic works like the famous *Dying Galatian* sculpture of Pergamon. So the answer to our first basic question is that the Celts used armour on a large scale, like all other peoples of antiquity, the only exception to this rule being some specific categories of warriors who fought naked for religious reasons.

The answer to the second question is probably the most difficult one to find. Organic materials like leather do not survive for centuries and tend to vanish over time. Metals, however, can easily survive for very long periods, which is why we have several examples of Celtic bronze cuirasses and iron chainmail but no surviving elements of leather armour. Iconography is not of great help in answering our question, since representations of Celtic warriors with armour are extremely rare. Personally, I think that the Celts surely also employed organic armour and not only bronze cuirasses or iron chainmail. However, leather or linen cuirasses would not have been as popular

Celtic blacksmith at work. (The *Trimatrici*)

Celtic blacksmith at work. (The *Trimatrici*)

as those made with metals. There are two main reasons for this: organic armour was not part of the Celtic military tradition, and the Celts were famous for their great capabilities in working metals and not their artefacts made with other materials. A Celtic warrior would have preferred fighting naked instead of using organic armour: for the Celts, armour was a synonym for metal, bronze or iron. Yet this general concept does not exclude the concrete possibility that the Celts also employed cuirasses made of leather or linen, which were probably much more common among the eastern Celts, who were influenced by the military practices of the Greek world. Another important consideration on this point brings us to the third question, where personally, I think that organic armour was a popular alternative to metal for the poorest warriors. Noble/ rich soldiers were generally equipped with personal protections made of bronze or iron, but these were too costly for the common peasants/farmers who were not professional warriors. As a result, we could say that the use of these two different kinds of armour corresponded to the personal economic situation of individual warriors. The poorest ones, albeit not fighting naked, probably did not have the ability to buy even organic armour made of leather or linen. One final consideration is of a practical nature, namely that wearing heavy armour made of metal was much simpler for noble warriorsas they fought from war chariots or mounted on horses. The common warrior, fighting as an infantryman, would have lost most of his mobility if wearing a bronze cuirass or iron chainmail.

At the beginning of the La Tène Period, Celtic armour mostly consisted of bronze discs worn over the chest to protect that vital part of the body. These were generally decorated with incisions and bosses, being quite light and easy to wear. The practice of wearing simple discs as body protection was very popular too among other contemporaries, including the Italic or Iberian peoples. In addition, noble/rich warrior

Celtic shield wall. (The *Ambiani*)

Meeting between two allied Celtic warriors. (The *Mediomatrici*)

could wear padded garments covered with leather and strongly reinforced by small bosses or discs made of bronze. These were sleeveless and generally reached the knee of the wearer, and sometimes the bronze bosses and discs could have a specific disposition in order to reproduce a decorative geometrical pattern. These leather garments were frequently worn in combination with the traditional Celtic waistbelt, which was quite large and made of bronze. Bronze greaves, rather simple in shape, continued to be used, albeit not on a large scale. There was a real revolution regarding Celtic armour around the end of the fifth century BC when the Celts invented chainmail. This armour soon became extremely popular in the Mediterranean world, being used on a large scale until the fall of the Roman Empire and later for most of the Middle Ages. The fact that the Celts invented the most effective and widespread kind of armour in the history of the world is another important confirmation of their absolute superiority as metal-workers. Like with helmets, the Romans soon understood the great potential of this Celtic military invention and introduced it into their own military forces.

Basically, a chainmail, known as *lorica hamata* by the Romans, is made of thousands of small iron rings linked together to form a mesh: the rings are interlocked in a formidable way, creating something similar to a knitted sweater. Depending on its dimensions, a chainmail is made up of 20,000 metal rings and weighs approximately 10kg. Celtic chainmail was generally sleeveless but had reinforcement panels for the shoulders, attached across the top of the back and held at the front by a bar and stud device. A double thong was stretched from the rings attached just above the inner corners of cut-outs to the outer corner of each of the reinforcement panels. The edges of the latter were bound with rawhide to create a raised border. The panels could have angled or rounded-off ends on the chest. Later Celtic chainmail started to have short sleeves, but this did not change their general shape. Around the end of the fifth century BC, while chainmail became extremely popular among the western Celts, those in the east started to employ organic armour made of leather or linen, clearly inspired by the cuirasses worn by the contemporary Greek hoplites/phalangists (such as the famous linen linothorax). While these protections for the body were not as effective as chainmail, they were much lighter and easier to produce, were perfect for the hot climate of the southern Balkans and cost much less than a metal corselet. The Celts did not change Greek patterns, and even included the pteruges (strips of leather worn with the armour to protect the upper arms and waist) in their own sets of armour. However, they usually decorated organic armour with their own peculiar patterns, painting linen cuirasses or making incisions on leather ones. This organic armour had reinforcement panels for the shoulders exactly like those for chainmail, with their panels sometimes made of leather rather than metal rings.

Chainmail or organic armour was worn over a Celtic warrior's everyday dress, which was quite practical and simple. Very often, however, chainmail was worn over some additional padded garment that was used to protect the wearer from potential wounds caused by the breaking of the metal rings, which could happen, for example, when chainmail was pierced by an arrow. Before describing the basic dress of a Celtic man, we should bear in mind that the practice of painting and tattooing bodies was extremely popular, especially in the British Isles. The Celts used woad (a plant) to produce a deep blue dye that was used for tattooing: body painting on the face, arms and torso had a ritual significance and showed an individual's trust in the gods. Celtic clothing was extremely colourful and was embroidered in a very peculiar way, with vertical and horizontal lines forming a distinctive decorative pattern that would later evolve to become the famous tartan. Bright colours and geometric motifs were something peculiar to the Celts, which made their clothing easily recognizable throughout the Ancient world. These colours were obtained from vegetables that were unknown by the Greeks and Romans, thus looking completely new to the latter. The ordinary clothing of a Celtic man/warrior included three elements: tunic, breeches and cloak (which was heavy for winter and light for summer). These were produced in brighter

Celtic warriors on the march. (The *Ambiani*)

Group of Celtic warriors with their chief. (The *Trimatrici*)

colours and had massive embroidering if worn by a rich/noble individual, while ordinary men had clothes with solid colours and no decorations. Cloaks were the most precious component of a Celtic man's wardrobe, together with the brooches that were used to keep them in the correct position. Wool was used to produce winter clothing, while linen was employed for summer, with silk and gold thread employed only to fabricate the dress of the richest nobles. In addition to the necklaces and brooches already described, Celtic men loved to wear other jewels such as bracelets or rings.

In addition to armour, all Celtic warriors used massive shields to protect themselves. These were also carried in battle by the poorest fighters and their use was a fundamental element of the Celtic tactics, together with the use of long slashing swords. Celtic shields are part of the category known as bodyshields, because they were long and large enough to protect a warrior from the shoulders to the ankles. The Celtic shields could have two different shapes, hexagonal or oval. Most had a central spine made of wood and a boss (*umbo*) made of metal in varying shapes, which were designed to reinforce the whole structure of the shield. Celtic shields were made of oak planks, which were chamfered to a thinner section towards the rim, while the wooden spine, swelling in the middle, was shaped in order to correspond with a round or oval cut-out in the shield centre. The strap-type metal boss crossed over the wider section of the spine and was riveted on the external surface of the shield, which, on both sides or only on the front, was entirely covered with leather that could be painted in various bright colours and have decorations of several kinds (always linked to Celtic religious beliefs). Bosses corresponded to the handle of the shield on the back and thus had a fundamental function in protecting the user's hand. Additional metal binding was frequently attached to the external edges of the shield in order to reinforce it. Decorative metal figures were often applied to the external surface, being combined with the painted decorations. Like many other elements of the Celtic *panoplia*, the oval shields were copied and adopted by the two fiercest enemies of the Celts: both the Greeks and the Romans introduced oval shields in their armies after encountering the Celts on the field of battle. Greek armies of the Hellenistic Period started to include a new category of 'medium' infantrymen, known as *thureophoroi*, which were equipped with Celtic oval shields and had no other personal protection except for a helmet. The Romans, meanwhile, adopted oval shields after reorganizing their legions according to the new manipular structure. The *scutum* (oval shield) continued to be used by the Roman legions until the reign of Augustus, while the *auxilia* (most of whom were of Celtic origins) continued to use it for at least another two centuries. Celtic cavalry, especially during the second half of the La Tène Period, started to employ smaller and round shields instead of the oval/hexagonal ones. These were built according to the same system described above, but were much more practical for use in the saddle. The cavalry could apparently also employ a smaller version of the hexagonal shield, the shape of which more or less resembled a square and which was much shorter than the proper hexagonal shield carried by infantrymen. In addition to normal shields, Celtic warlords also had parade ones that were not employed in battle: these had more or less the same shape as the others, but were made of wood entirely covered by a bronze sheet on the external surface. The bronze sheet was richly adorned with sculpted motifs, decorative applications and gems. Two of these parade shields have been found in Britain: one in the Thames at Battersea and another in the Witham in Lincolnshire.

The main offensive weapon of the Celts was the long slashing sword, which would later be adopted by the Roman cavalry and called the *spatha*. This was used by all categories of Celtic warriors, not only heavy cavalrymen. Celtic mercenaries were renowned in the Ancient world as excellent swordsmen acting as shock troops on the

Celtic warlord with his retainers. (The *Trimatrici*)

battlefield. The blade of the La Tène Period swords had a distinct elongated leaf shape, being double-edged and having a square-kink or shallow 'V' point (with sides drawn at an angle of 45 degrees to the axis of the blade). The tang of these swords (the internal part of the handle, made of metal but covered with organic material) swells sharply, to a point of greatest width that is just below its centre. The ricasso (the unsharpened length of blade just above the handle of the sword) was very short and had a notch that varied greatly in depth. Sword handles were made of wood or leather and generally had the form of an 'X', thus continuing the previous pattern of the 'antennae' swords. The handle was completed by a pommel, which was connected to the tang with a rivet-hole. The blade itself measured about 60-90cm in length and was by now entirely made from iron or steel. At the beginning of the La Tène Period, Celtic swords were generally about 60cm long and thus had more or less the same dimensions of those used by the Greeks and Romans, but from the third century BC, the length started to increase and reached 90cm by the time Caesar launched his campaigns of conquest in Gaul. At the same time as blades became longer, the points started to be increasingly rounded. This shape of the point clearly demonstrates that the weapons were used for slashing and not for thrusting. Blades generally had a broad neck, with the greatest width usually being low down towards the point. Swords were carried in iron scabbards, richly decorated with incisions and/or bosses. Scabbards reproduced the general shape of the blade and were constructed from two plates: the front one, slightly wider than the back, was folded over it along the sides. Each scabbard was reinforced by a decorated band around the top and a sculpted chip at the bottom. Scabbards were generally

Celtic infantrymen in close formation. (The *Trimatrici*)

suspended on the right hip from a sword belt made of leather or from a chain of linked iron rings (the latter being a distinctive element of the Celtic panoply). The sword was suspended from the waistbelt by means of a metal loop located on the back face of the scabbard. In addition to swords, Celtic warriors continued to use daggers as secondary weapons. These were very short but had quite large blades (with a central ridge acting as reinforcement) and could have different models of handle. Daggers could have very broad blades with a distinct triangular shape, but smaller models were also very popular. All of them had a triangular point, thus being deadly weapons when used in close combat.

Spears were another important component of the Celtic warriors' personal equipment, being employed as thrusting weapons by both infantry and cavalry. Their points were by now entirely made of iron and had an elongated shape. During the early

Celtic infantry in defensive position. (The *Ambiani*)

La Tène Period they were much larger, becoming smaller by the time of Julius Caesar. The most common shape had its edges curving inwards from the belly of the blade to its tip. Butt spikes, also made of leather, were of socketed or tanged fitting. An average Celtic spear was about 2.5 m long. The Celts apparently used also some parade spears, which were used as standards on the field of battle: these were much longer and larger than the normal spears, having points with many decorative holes and/or undulating edges. Parade spears were not the only kind of insignia employed by the Celts, as there were also more conventional ones made of bronze: these usually reproduced the same sacred animals that were placed on the top of parade helmets (boars, deer, wolves, foxes, bears, horses and bulls). Each tribal 'clan' had its own insignia, which was strongly linked to the gods protecting the familiar group. It seems that the famous eagles of the Roman legions derived from these Celtic standards. Celtic warriors also had musical instruments to communicate tactical signals during battle: these could be traditional horns or the peculiar Celtic trumpet known as the carnyx (which was made of bronze, being extremely long and having the mouth in the shape of a sacred animal's head). Each carnyx trumpet had a movable jaw and a wooden tongue, which were used to produce a raucous rattling sound. Generally speaking, Celtic warriors did not like missile weapons very much, as in a society that considered personal courage as the most important value, throwing missiles from a distance was perceived as a cowardly way of fighting. As a result of this conception, bows and slings were very rarely employed, and on a small scale. Javelins, however, were more popular and were used on a larger scale, especially by light cavalrymen (who rode against the enemy at the beginning of the battle and used javelins to harass their opponents). Celtic warriors preferred engaging enemies in single combat, transforming battles into a large series of duels taking place at the same time. As a result, the use of missile weapons like bows and slings would only occur during siege operations. Celtic light troops, both foot or mounted, were generally equipped with small round or rectangular shields with no central spine.

Chapter 10

Celtic Warfare and Battle Tactics

At the beginning of a battle, Celtic infantrymen were deployed in great masses according to their own tribal provenance. Before charging against the enemy, they used all their weapons of 'psychological warfare' in order to spread terror in the opponents' ranks. First of all they slashed the air with their long swords and poured abuse on the enemy, producing a great noise with terrible war cries and by banging their weapons on the large shields. This frightening spectacle was completed by the tossing of standards and the terrific braying of horns and trumpets. During this initial phase several 'champions' (chosen warriors) usually came out of the ranks and engaged in duels with the best fighters of the opposing army: the outcome of these single combats usually had a deep impact over the morale of the two armies deployed on the field, so were not merely a secondary part of a battle's early phase. After some time in these preliminary activities, the Celtic warriors charged the enemy en masse, continuing to scream and slash the air with their swords, hoping by this to cause a break in the opponents' line due to panic. Shortly before investing the front line of the enemy, Celtic warriors equipped with javelins (who were deployed in the front lines) used their missile weapons to break the integrity of the enemy formation. Once in direct contact with the enemy, each Celtic warrior engaged in a duel with an opponent, with these individual clashes decided by the physique and swordsmanship of the fighters and lasting anything from a few seconds to several minutes. Generally speaking, Celtic tactics were extremely simple: if the kind of frontal assault described above was repulsed, Celtic warriors had no alternative but to launch another one. These frontal charges would continue until the enemy army was broken or the Celtic fighters became exhausted. Very frequently, after a failed assault, the Celts completely lost their morale and were crushed by an effective counter–attack mounted by their enemies. The chances of victory for a Celtic army were strongly related to the success of the first charge: if this failed, Celtic warriors generally lost their impetus and were prone to abandon the battlefield in rout. The terrific frontal assaults of the Celts caused serious problems for their enemies, including the Romans at the River Allia, but the latter soon learned how to stop them with javelin volleys and by alternating fresh troops in the front line.

Infantry, however, was not the only component of Celtic armies. Light troops (both foot or mounted) had little tactical importance and were mostly employed to harass the enemy during the early phases of a combat, or else during guerrilla operations conducted on broken terrain. Heavy cavalry, however, played a major role in Celtic warfare, as did war chariots. The Celtic war chariot from the La Tène Period was a two-wheeled vehicle with an oblong platform secured above the axle at the centre of its length. On each side of the platform were side panels formed by double semi-circular bows of wood that were filled in with inserts of composite material (including wood, leather and wickerwork). The trace reins were attached to the axle housing by metal lugs in order to transfer the pull directly to the wheels. The centre pole was connected both to the axle housing and the platform. In general, due to its peculiar structure and construction, the Celtic war chariot was quite light but also stable enough to be employed on a partly broken terrain. From a tactical point of view, the Celts did not use their war chariots to charge the enemy directly: they were more like mobile platforms, from which a warlord could throw his javelins against the enemy during the early phases of combat. When the proper fighting started, each warlord dismounted from his chariot in order to fight in the front line as a normal infantryman. The servants of nobles also acted as chariot drivers, transporting the weapons of their lord and taking care of the horses. The use of war chariots was apparently progressively abandoned throughout Celtic Europe, except for the British Isles. When Caesar's legionaries landed in southern Britain, they were greatly surprised by the presence of so many war chariots and initially had serious difficulties in countering them. The majority of Celtic cavalrymen, being noble warriors, had heavy personal equipment, including helmet and chainmail; their offensive weapons included javelins (used during the first phase of a combat) plus spear and long slashing sword (employed during the decisive phase of charge/close combat). Celtic saddles were constructed with a pommel on each corner of the seat unit in order to have a higher degree of stability. Both bar and jointed snaffled bits were used to control the horse.

Bibliography

Primary sources
Ammianus Marcellinus, *Rerum Gestarum*
Appianus, *Gallic History*
Appianus, *Hannibalic War*
Appianus, *Illyrian Wars*
Appianus, *Wars in Spain*
Dio Cassius, *Roman History*
Diodorus Siculus, *Library of History*
Herodotus, *The Histories*
Julius Caesar, *Commentaries on the Gallic War*
Marcus Annaeus Lucanus, *Pharsalia*
Pausanias, *Description of Greece*
Pliny the Elder, *The Natural History*
Polybius, *Histories*
Silius Italicus, *Punica*
Strabo, *Geography*
Tacitus, *Agricola*
Tacitus, *The Annals*
Tacitus, *The Histories*
Titus Livius, *The History of Rome*
Xenophon, *Hellenica*

Secondary sources
Allen, S., *Celtic Warrior 300 BC – AD 100* (Osprey Publishing, 2001)
Baker, P., *Armies and Enemies of Imperial Rome* (Wargames Research Group, 1981)
Connolly, P., *Greece and Rome at War* (Frontline Books, 1981)
Cunliffe, B., *The Ancient Celts* (Penguin Books, 1997)
Dougherty, M.J., *Celts: the History and Legacy of one of the Oldest Cultures in Europe* (Amber Books, 2015)
Ellis, P., *The Celts: A History* (Running Press, 2003)
Gorelik, K., *Warriors of Eurasia* (Montvert Publishing, 1995)
Head, D., *Armies of the Macedonian and Punic Wars* (Wargames Research Group, 1982)
King, J., *Kingdoms of the Celts* (Blandford, 2000)
Konstam, A., *Historical Atlas of the Celtic World* (Mercury Books, 2003)
Newark, T., *Ancient Celts* (Concord Publications, 1997)
Newark, T., *Barbarians* (Concord Publications, 1998)
Newark, T., *Ancient Armies* (Concord Publications, 2000)

Newark, T., *Warlord Armies* (Concord Publications, 2004)

Webber, C., *The Thracians 700 BC-AD 46* (Osprey Publishing, 2001)

Wilcox, P., *Rome's Enemies 1: Germanics and Dacians* (Osprey Publishing, 1982)

Wilcox, P., *Rome's Enemies 2: Gallic and British Celts* (Osprey Publishing, 1985)

Winter, H.E., *A History of the Celts* (The Book Guild, 2004)

The Re-enactors who Contributed to this Book

Confraternita del Leone/Historia Viva

La *Confraternita del Leone* è un'associazione culturale di ricostruzione storica, con l'obiettivo di studiare, rivivere e divulgare la storia lombarda, con particolare attenzione a quella di Brescia e delle popolazioni che l'hanno abitata nei secoli. Le ricerche dei nostri studiosi spaziano senza limiti nella ricca e complessa storia locale, concentrando l'aspetto rievocativo e didattico sui periodi dal IV al I secolo a.C. in cui furono protagonisti Reti, Celti e Romani, quindi sul secolo VIII dei Longobardi, sull'età dei Comuni e delle Signorie del XII e XIII secolo e infine sul XVII secolo e l'epoca dei Buli sotto la Repubblica di Venezia. La ricerca storica della *Confraternita del Leone* si articola su tre differenti e complementari piattaforme di studio, la cui finalità è raggiungere dei risultati di globalità analitica in grado di estrinsecare degli spaccati storici di corretta filologicità e, ove possibile, di assoluto realismo e scientificità: istituto di ricerca storica, laboratori di archeologia sperimentale e accademia di antiche arti marziali occidentali. Nel partecipare ad eventi storici la *Confraternita del Leone* allestisce un accampamento di circa 500 metri quadrati, dispone di vari antichi mestieri dimostrativi con artigiani all'opera tra cui il fabbro con la forgia, la tessitura a telaio, la macinazione di cereali, l'usbergaro, lo speziale, il cerusico, la zecca, il cambiavalute, il cacciatore, l'arcaio, lo scrivano, l'avvocato e il fabbricante di candele; in battaglia sono schierati arcieri, balestrieri, fanteria, ariete, trabucchi e mantelletti.

Contacts:
E-mail: confraternitadelleone@gmail.com
Website: http://www.confraternitaleone.com/

Historia Viva è un istituto di ricerca storica e archeologia sperimentale che, mediante lo studio delle fonti e l'attività sul campo in sinergia con rievocatori e ricercatori storici, realizza eventi culturali, festival, mostre, rassegne e propone spaccati di vita quotidiana, marziale e civile, dal neolitico fino alla metà del secolo scorso. Gli eventi realizzati affiancano alla componente ricostruttiva di momenti del passato elementi musicali e di gastronomia coeva, che concorrono a introdurre il pubblico in una interazione sensoriale completa che dà al visitatore un arricchimento culturale attivo, non subìto esternamente ma vissuto interiormente. *Historia Viva* collabora con produzioni documentaristiche, cinematografiche e di pubblicazioni storiche per quel che concerne gli aspetti legati alla marzialità e la contestualizzazione dei periodi analizzati.

Contacts:

E-mail: hveventi@gmail.com

Website: https://historiaviva.info/

Contoutos Atrebates

The association *Contoutos Atrebates* was created at the end of 2015, with the ambitious objective of reconstructing the daily life of one of Gaul's most important Celtic tribes: the Atrebates, who lived in northern France around present-day Arras. The Atrebates were part of the Celtic communities living in "Gallia Belgica" and their name meant "colonists" in Celtic language. After being defeated by Julius Caesar, these fierce warriors did not accept to surrender and thus later joined the great Gallic Revolt of 52 BC against the Romans. After the Battle of Alesia, the surviving members of the Atrebates negotiated a truce with the Romans and were permitted to abandon Gaul in order to create a new settlement in southern Britannia. In southern Britain the Atrebates founded a new kingdom that remained an ally of Rome for several decades; around 40 AD their territories were invaded by the Catuvellauni, this event being the main "casus belli" for the Roman invasion of Britannia of some years later. The *Contoutos Atrebates* tries to reconstruct the costumes and weapons of the Atrebates people during the crucial period of the Gallic Wars, but also from previous periods: our activities do include also the reenactment of some important aspects related to daily life of a Celtic community, like cooking or producing artefacts. We are interested to any kind of collaboration dealing with Celtic reenactment from a scientific point of view.

Contacts:

E-mail: ctatrebates@yahoo.fr

Website: https://www.facebook.com/contoutos.atrebate

G.A.S.A.C.

L'Associazione *G.A.S.A.C.* (Gruppo per l'Archeologia Sperimentale di Arte Celtica) da diversi lustri promuove la conoscenza e la valorizzazione della cultura e dell'arte del popolo celtico. Presidente e "motore" dell'Associazione culturale *G.A.S.A.C.* è Giuseppe Stucchi, nato nel 1949 a Trezzo sull'Adda. L'artista, stimolato da una passione innata, tramite l'Archeologia Sperimentale ha generato una vasta raccolta di oggetti e tuttora dispone di un'ampia collezione di alcune centinaia di pezzi (di cui fanno parte oggetti in bronzo, ferro, rame, argento ed oro). Riproducendo spade, elmi, collari e "torques" tutti realizzati rispettando le antiche tecniche costruttive artigianali celtiche. Nella sua sperimentazione l'artista è accompagnato da collaboratori tecnici ed archeologi che lo aiutano e lo supportano nella ricerca, nella raccolta di documentazione e nella realizzazione di nuove opere. Gli incontri avuti, nel recente passato, con i più autorevoli esperti di celtismo hanno affinato il lavoro di ricerca facendo produrre manufatti di esclusiva esecuzione e di grande pregio. La finalità dell'Associazione *G.A.S.A.C.* è la divulgazione della cultura e della storia del popolo celtico nostro antenato e di far apprezzare il suo patrimonio di conoscenze nella sua specifica originalità. L'Associazione auspica che attraverso la divulgazione si possa arrivare alla conservazione culturale di questo grande tesoro rappresentato dalla cultura del popolo celtico. Pertanto essa si prefigge di raggiungere questo obiettivo attraverso l'Archeologia Sperimentale, tramite metodologie didattico/illustrative che stimolino il desiderio di conoscenza di tutti coloro che visitano le mostre culturali allestite dall'associazione.

Contacts:

Website: http://www.arteceltica.it/

Les Ambiani

The *Ambiani* is a French association gathering enthusiasts of Celtic Period. Composed by professional archaeologists and amateurs of history, the association reenacts a group of warriors and artisans from the Gallic Wars period (which took place around the half of the I century BC). The Ambiani were a Celtic tribe that inhabited in the valley of the Somme in "Gallia Belgica", nowadays in Picardie (in the north of France). Our reconstructions are based on the most recent discoveries and try, as much as possible, to focus on the material culture of the people of the region of Amiens from where the association takes its name. Our activities include animations in the form of pedagogical workshops (presentation of the weapons, training of the infantrymen, cavalry, fighting in duels and in battle formations, religious ceremonies) and in workshops showing a series of activities from the domestic sphere to more specialized craft productions (cooking, pottery, bone work, weaving, forging, minting coins). The *Ambiani* group works in collaboration with many specialists to develop and improve reconstructions, in order to follow the evolution of research and conduct experiments. We also created a small archaeo-site in Pont-Rémy, near Abbeville, with buildings based on archaeological discoveries and have conducted an ambitious project involving the reconstruction of a Gallo-Roman barge.

Contacts:

E-mail: secretariat@les-ambiani.fr

Website: http://www.les-ambiani.com/

Facebook: https://www.facebook.com/Les-Ambiani-729215287167804/

Les Mediomatrici

In 2009 Thierry Chataigneau founded the Celtic Iron Age historical reenactment group *Mediomatrici*, with Cédric Mangin (vice-president), Jean-Marc Hein (treasurer) and Denis Aubry (secretary) in Alsace (France). The name *Mediomatrici* has been chosen to commemorate this real historical people living in Alsace, two thousand years ago. The *Mediomatrici* is an association dedicated to the La Tène Period; it has, in fact, the main objective of presenting to the public the way of life of the Gauls during the I century BC. The *Mediomatrici* are dedicated to experimental archaeology, which allowed them to publish two studies (one devoted to Celtic helmets of the "Novo Mesto type" and the other to the Gallic harvester "Vallus") in the French magazine "Histoire Antique et Médiévale" by Editions Faton. The *Mediomatrici* present the combat techniques and Gallic armament of final La Tène Period to the public during historical events, in archaeological museums and in schools (in France but also in other countries). We also present Gallic crafts: dyeing, weaving, leather work and fabrication of chainmails. As an example of experimental archaeology, the paintings on the shields of the *Mediomatrici* warriors have been realized with self-made milk painting containing natural pigments. The motives painted on the shields are taken from illustrations reproduced on Celtic Iron Age coins. Currently, Thierry Chataigneau is publishing a historical Gallic soap-opera dedicated to the Mediomatrici during the Gallic Wars, for the magazine "Histoire de l'Antiquité à nos Jours" by Editions Faton. The group has already participated to many documentaries devoted to the Gauls and their history.

Contacts:

Website: http://mediomatrici.gaulois.over-blog.com and http://mediomatrici-gaulois. eklablog.com

Facebook: https://www.facebook.com/Mediomatrici and https://www.facebook.com/ durnacos.nertomari

Les Trimatrici

The proto-historic reenactment troupe *Trimatrici* is attached to the MJC of Gerstheim, in Bas-Rhin (France). Today it includes more than thirty people: archaeologists, craftsmen, students and simple amateurs. These are strongly linked together by a common interest for Gallic civilization and by a desire to present it in the liveliest way possible. With this in mind, we try to reconstruct as faithfully as possible the craftsmanship, weapons and tactics of combat of Celts; more in general we aim at creating a reconstruction of the Gallic life as it was near the end of Celtic independence (more specifically during the period of the Gallic Wars. The name of our association derives from the Médiomatrici and Triboci, two extremely important Celtic tribes of Gaul. Our services are modulated according to the circumstances (like presentations in schools or in archaeo-sites) but usually we install a camp in which the public can follow the various workshops that we propose. These include craft activities, as well as the presentation of Gallic armour from La Tène Period. Following our experiments on combat techniques, we offer demonstrations at various times of the day that are fun and educational. We operate throughout France and abroad, depending on our availability.

Contacts:

Website: http://trimatrici.fr/

Facebook: https://www.facebook.com/trimatrici

Teuta Arverni

The troupe *Teuta Arverni*, formed according to the French Association Law 1901, brings together women, men and children who are all passionate about Celtic history. Thanks to historical evocation and scientific reconstruction, we present the life of the Arverne people in the I century BC and especially during the Gallic Wars that opposed many Celtic tribes to the Roman legions of Julius Caesar. In particular, we recreate the following components of the Celtic world: the aristocracy and the military; the civil world, with particular attention to artisans and peasants; the daily life of a tribal community (including cooking, hygiene and education). Our works and reflections are based on the discoveries made on the "oppida" and major sites of the Arvernes (Corent, Gergovie, Gondola, Aulnat-Gandaillat) but also on the writings of ancient authors and on the most recent researches published by historians and archaeologists. Broadly speaking the *Teuta Arverni* wish to reconstruct the Celtic world with an innovative approach that is much more in line with recent scientific and archaeological data, by correcting a number of clichés and received ideas that are still largely maintained by the media.

Contacts:

Website: http://www.teuta-arverni.com/

Teuta Osismi

Teuta Osismi is a historical re-enactment association, born in 2009, which aims to show how the Osismi people lived between the III and I century BC. It focuses on both military and civil life. The Osismi were a Celtic tribe living in the western half of modern Brittany and they belonged to the so-called Armorican Confederation (known in Celtic language as "the country that faces the Ocean"). Our association mostly aims to democratize History and Archaeology: for this purpose, we participate to events organized by museums and local institutions. These performances are mostly made in camps, with about 20 people including craftsmen and women but also a dozen of warriors. Our camp is divided in "workshops", each one showing a different kind of artisan work. *Teuta Osismi* has also participated to many cultural events, such as movies about the "Vénètes", short films and picture exhibitions with a historical perspective. The association also offers many animations for kids, adults and elders. These include reconstructions of daily life in a Gallic camp, demos of object-crafting with antique methods, initiations to some workshops (weaving, forge, leather, jewels, cooking), simulations of martial formations and demonstrations with our members. Our members gather each month to experiment new scientific hypotheses on Gallic fighting, by using different weapons according to their technical characteristics. Furthermore we cooperate with "Aremorica", another well-known association working on crafts from the proto-historical period to the Gallo-Roman one.

Contacts:

Email: teutaosismi@gmail.com

Website: http://www.osismi.fr/

Facebook: https://www.facebook.com/teutaosismi/

Index